MW00974370

What Others Are Saying

Looking at it from outside the glass cabinet of a bakery, it appeared as a flaky pastry with possible jelly filling inside. However, when I bit into it, I discovered this fresh pastry enclosed a delicious combination of fruit and meat. I immediately wanted more. That was similar to the experience I had when reading *Big Doors Swing on Small Hinges*. Dr. Mardis serves the Scriptures in bite-size segments for daily ingestion, but each day they are both exciting and nourishing, fun and filling. It was hard to resist the temptation to look ahead to see what was on the menu for the next day. People of every season of life will find this book deep and delicious!

—Michael Cloer, pastor, Englewood Baptist Church

Insightful, unique, and challenging are the words that describe Roger Mardis' book, *Big Doors Swing On Small Hinges*. There is no telling what doors God may choose to open in your life when you take this 31-day challenge.

—Ronnie Floyd, pastor, Cross Church

Roger Mardis has written an encouraging book around the conjunction *but!* The use of "doors" as a way to look at situations from Noah to our Lord is an insightful and helpful walk through Scripture that will prove to be a blessing to the reader. All of us can benefit from recognizing the doors of opportunity and understand they can swing on a small hinge like *but!*

—Sammy Gilbreath, director of the office of evangelism,
Alabama State Board of Missions

Roger Mardis has written not just a very clever book but a very convicting one as well. As you turn the pages to walk through these various "doors," you will be encouraged and reminded that the Lord has indeed "set before us an open door" and you will be challenged by the fact that big doors do indeed swing on small hinges like you and me and often seemingly insignificant circumstances that unfold before us. Read it and reap.

—O. S. Hawkins, president/CEO,
GuideStone Financial Resources

For those of us who love reading devotional books, pastor Roger Mardis has done us a tremendous favor. He has taken an often-used little conjunction and given us a biographical and topical/textual tour of the Bible. That is the essence of *Big Doors Swing On Small Hinges.* You will be enriched by this excursion through God's Word, and you will learn from the artful exposition offered by this Bible-preaching and teaching pastor. I wholeheartedly recommend reading this book. You will love it!

—Rick Lance, executive director,
Alabama State Board of Missions, treasurer,
Alabama Baptist Convention

I have known Roger Mardis for many years. His dad was a groomsman in my wedding. Roger once served on my staff while I was pastor at Kirby Woods Baptist Church in Memphis, TN. Roger is a godly man and an outstanding student of Scripture. He has spent myriad hours putting together this devotional guide. This volume contains inspiration, encouragement, challenge, and warning. Read it carefully and heed it fervently. Your "doors" will be better, easier, and safer if you will.

—Bob Pitman, evangelist

I'm so thankful for this book and the ministry of Roger Mardis. He has been a personal friend for over 20 years, and I thank God for his passion for Jesus and his impact on so many people. I know the Lord will use this book to inspire many in their walk with the Lord.

—Vance Pitman, pastor, Hope Church

In this book, author Roger Mardis literally opens a door for the reader that connects our circumstances with the powerful purposes of God. This helpful, practical, and inspirational devotional journey will encourage and challenge your heart. As a pastor, I always appreciate resources like this one that allow God's Word to touch people where they live—and this book does exactly that with clarity and conviction. Enjoy the journey!

—Danny Sinquefield, pastor,
Faith Baptist Church, Bartlett, Tennessee

If you are looking for a book that will not only bless you greatly but also remind you of the truthfulness of every Word of Scripture, Roger Mardis has the book for you. I recommend this new work, *Big Doors Swing on Small Hinges,* and you will find refreshment and encouragement there. Dr. Mardis pours his pastoral heart into these pages, and I think that you need to read this book; in fact, I insist on it.

—Michael Spradlin, president,
Mid-America Baptist Theological Seminary

When Roger Mardis has something to say, the world needs to stop and listen. He writes convincingly in this book of the long-range implications of shortsighted decisions. I know him, trust him, and admire him—and Roger's comments are worthy of our serious consideration. You will find this book to be packed with thoughtful, relevant commentary on a topic that touches each one of us.

—Andrew Westmoreland, president, Samford University

BIG DOORS SWING ON SMALL HINGES

A Little Word Can Make a Big Difference

ROGER D. MARDIS

WESTBOW®
PRESS
A DIVISION OF THOMAS NELSON
& ZONDERVAN

WestBow Press books may be ordered through booksellers or by contacting:

WestBow Press
A Division of Thomas Nelson & Zondervan
1663 Liberty Drive
Bloomington, IN 47403
www.westbowpress.com
1 (866) 928-1240

ISBN: 978-1-4908-3819-9 (sc)
ISBN: 978-1-4908-3820-5 (hc)
ISBN: 978-1-4908-3818-2 (e)

Library of Congress Control Number: 2014909364

Printed in the United States of America.

WestBow Press rev. date: 6/3/2014

To Michelle…

This book is dedicated to my wife, Michelle. I am a blessed man living a blessed life because the Lord blessed me with you. It's a joy to do life and ministry with you.

All my love – all my life,

Roger

Contents

Foreword

Most of us recognize that small things often have large consequences. A tiny splinter can create great pain. A minute cancer cell can destroy someone's health. On the other hand, a small act of kindness can encourage a downcast heart. Many times, God uses the small word or deed to make a big impact. Indeed, small things can alter the trajectory of our lives.

In his new book, *Big Doors Swing on Small Hinges*, veteran pastor Roger Mardis has given us a gift by pointing out some of the small "hinges" upon which many significant biblical events have turned. As I read these chapters, I found myself riveted by the amazingly important episodes in the Bible prefaced by the three-letter conjunction *but*. These involved everyone from Noah, David, and Daniel to the Lord Himself. Like a hammer steadily driving in a nail blow by blow, each chapter confirms that great experiences with long-lasting, even eternal results turn on the small "hinges" of seemingly inconsequential actions or words.

Reading this work, you will find that there are no small decisions or actions in life. Everything we think, do, or say is of big importance. In fact, the results follow us for the rest of our lives. As my predecessor, Adrian Rogers, often said, "We reap what we sow, we reap more than we sow, and we reap after we sow."

I like this work for several reasons. The thirty-one-day format is very doable, even for those of us who consider ourselves extremely busy. The book is also full of truth from which anyone can benefit. It could be used handily in a Bible study, a Sunday school class, or a discipleship group. My spiritual life is better for having digested the truths this book presents.

The author is a man of God and a friend of mine. I encourage you to read and pray through these insightful chapters. Come to grips with the significance of every small action, thought, and word. Allow Roger to show you that a little word can, in fact, make a big difference.

3 John 2,

Steve Gaines, PhD
senior pastor, Bellevue Baptist Church
Memphis, Tennessee

Preface

After more than thirty years of pastoral ministry, I've read my fair share of books and heard hundreds, if not thousands, of sermons, lectures, and speeches. During this time I've often written down a quote, a pithy statement, an illustration, or a sermon idea. Never did it cross my mind to document these sources so I wouldn't later be accused of plagiarizing someone else's idea.

I don't pretend that all the material in this book is original with me, but if I've found a bullet that will fit my gun, I've fired away. As a fellow preacher once said, "I've milked from a lot of cows but made my own butter." I like that, or perhaps I should say, I'm like that.

The goal of this book is not to offer original thought but to encourage fellow pilgrims in this journey we call life. I hope you'll read not with a critical eye, but with a burdened heart and a teachable spirit.

Acknowledgments

This book, like any other, wasn't the work of just the author. Many people contributed much to make *Big Doors Swing on Small Hinges* happen. I hope I don't leave anyone out, but I feel indebted to the following for their efforts:

- Cheryl Bellomy has been my assistant for the last thirteen years. Her work on this manuscript has been a "long and winding road." Thanks, Cheryl!
- Agape Baptist Church of Scottsboro, Alabama, is where I work, worship, and serve. I so appreciate the encouragement and faithfulness of church members, who heard each of these lessons firsthand.
- Carol Caudle is an amazing lady and a gifted artist. I am so glad my wife suggested I use her to illustrate the book. Her work is awesome.
- Terry Brown and his staff at the Ora Byram Allison Library at Mid-America Baptist Theological Seminary provided research and support for which I am deeply thankful.
- Harold Anderson, a friend from school days, encouraged me to write this book. He gave me the challenge and supported me through this process. I greatly appreciate his encouragement and friendship.
- The staff at WestBow Publishers has been extremely supportive. The professionalism and hard work of these people have been a great blessing. Thank you, team.
- Last but not least, this book was penned for the glory and honor of our Lord Jesus. It is a joy to serve Him.

Sola Dei Gloria,

Roger D. Mardis
Scottsboro, Alabama

Thirty-One Amazing Doors

At the beginning of each chapter, you will see one of the world's famous (or not-so-famous) doors. Some of these doors are at the entrances of familiar landmarks. Others are internal doors, and you may discover doors you've never heard of, much less walked through.

These doors are found in cities like Washington, D.C., London, Rome, Munich, and Annapolis. Others are at the entrances to famous cathedrals. You'll also see ancient wooden doors from throughout Italy. You will find thirty-one doors in all.

As I was preparing this manuscript, my wife suggested that I ask our friend, Carol Caudle, to draw these doors as illustrations for the book. As you see Carol's work, you'll know why we asked her. She is largely self-taught but obviously has a gift from our Lord. I encourage you to learn more about her work.

I have noted where these doors are located. What I've learned in my study is that the famous and fancy—just like the unknown and plain—all swing on relatively small hinges.

Together, let's open doors and in the process learn some of life's crucial lessons.

"As the door turns on its hinges ..." (Proverbs 26:14).

Introduction

I grew up in a small, cozy northwest Alabama town called Florence. This beautiful stop on the Tennessee River is your average Southern city. People there love to hunt, fish, golf, play sports, and go to church.

Florence is not known for much but has a few nice features. It is the hometown of blues singer W. C. Handy, the childhood home of British Open champion Stewart Cink, and the geographical home of the University of North Alabama and college football's Division II national championship game.

In Florence, you can find some great eateries. Trowbridge's has been serving ice cream, chicken salad, and pimento cheese sandwiches for eighty years. Bunyan's BBQ has a slaw dog that will make your tongue slap your jaws, and I still think that the filet at Dale's is at the top of most lists.

But something happened in Florence from 1918 to 1924 that would change the town for good. During that time, the federal government built a dam on the river between Florence and Muscle Shoals. The towering Wilson Dam project established a national standard for waterways and hydroelectric plants.

According to records of the US Army Corps of Engineers, the Wilson Dam was the most ambitious American public works project of the period. This massive structure, 137 feet high and more than 4,500 feet long, required the excavation of 1.5 million cubic yards of earth and rock and used over 1.3 million cubic yards of concrete. At ninety-four feet, this massive lock lift established a world record and remains the highest in the Tennessee Valley Authority system.

On many nights in my teen years, my friends and I would walk the concrete of Wilson Dam. We would go there after large rains to watch the spillways open. We would watch a barge or a tugboat being lifted or lowered through the lock. But the one memory that stands out most is seeing the dam's massive doors open once all the water had been dropped. These huge doors swing on relatively small hinges. I'm sure the engineers who constructed the doors would laugh at my calling these mechanisms hinges, but that's essentially what they are.

Never in my wildest dreams did I think that these journeys to Wilson Dam would inspire this book. However, since then I have seen the truth of my early observation. Whether in a bank building, a factory, an airport hanger, or a home, doors swing on comparatively small hinges.

Years ago at a pastors' conference in Jacksonville, Florida, I heard one of the speakers say, "You need to notice the *buts* of the Scripture, for they just might be a turning point in a life, in a story, or in a situation." He went on to say that "big doors swing on small hinges."

I've never forgotten that statement, and through the years in my preaching ministry, my study, and my Bible reading, I have tried to note the use of the word *but*. This little word is often the hinge on which a story is about to turn. Sometimes the story changes for the better, but sometimes it changes for the worse. Whether the change is beneficial or detrimental, it all starts with *but*.

Over the next thirty-one days, I want to lead you on a journey involving several Old and New Testament personalities and their stories, all of which hinged on the small word *but*. As you examine their lives, you will be reminded that your daily decisions, good or bad, may be the hinge on which your story—your life—changes. It was true that night in Jacksonville, it is true today at Wilson Dam, and it will be true for all of us: big doors swing on small hinges.

London, England

But Noah

Genesis 6:1–13

The word *but* is a conjunction. At times it may be used as a preposition or as an adverb, but primarily it is a joining word. It can mean "except," "however," "nevertheless," or "on the other hand." It is used in conversation or in writing to contrast situations or statements. For instance, we might say, "It has been a beautiful day but now it is cold and rainy."

In the Bible, this word is used on several occasions to indicate that the tide has turned in a situation or to compare people and events. This little word helps us make or see a contrast. Noticing the *buts* in Scripture can be helpful.

The first such hinge that we will see is found in Genesis. Stop for a moment and read Genesis 6:1–13. From these verses and others in Genesis, it's easy to figure out what is going on.

- There is a population explosion (6:1).
- There is a lack of respect for God's principles for marriage (6:1–4).
- There is a sense of utter corruption (6:5, 11–12).
- True believers are a minority.
- Violence has become widespread (6:11, 13).
- The arts and industry are expanding (4:16–22).
- Crime, including murder and homicide, is increasing (4:23–24).

The words *corruption, wickedness, disobedience,* and *compromise* sum up the situation. We are talking about the days of Noah, but the circumstances sound eerily similar to our own.

God saw all that was happening (6:5). He saw the utter depravity of man's heart. The Lord felt pain (6:6) and was heavily grieved. He wished He had never made man. The Lord said He was going to blot out man from the face of the earth (6:7). God had been patient (6:3) but now it was time for man to be punished.

But Noah found favor in the Lord's eyes (6:8).

How can we best describe Noah or how should we view him? I suggest four characteristics, and I hope they are true of you.

Noah Was a Believer

Noah experienced God's grace. Noah is not a minor character in the story of redemption. He is mentioned some fifty times in nine Bible books. Genesis 6:9 says Noah was a righteous man, and Hebrews 11:7 tells us he lived by faith.

Noah's righteousness did not come from his good works. His works were the byproduct of a heart made righteous. Noah's righteousness, like Abraham's, was God's answer to his faith. He believed God and as a result was made right. In fact, being in the ark is a glorious illustration of our being in Christ.

The biblical word *grace* does not refer to some kind of charm or to a disposition. It refers to God's unmerited favor. His grace reaches out to lost and ruined humanity, providing His love, kindness, and mercy. We receive something we don't deserve.

Noah Was a Worker

The Bible says that Noah built an ark. God told him why (6:13), how (6:14–16), and who (6:18–21), and this believer turned worker did all God said (6:22).

The test of whether one has been born again is a changed life. It is true that we cannot do anything to be saved except trust Jesus as

Lord and Savior, but it is equally true that we cannot be saved and do nothing. James said that kind of faith is worthless.

When Saul of Tarsus met Christ on that Damascus road, he immediately asked, "What do you want me to do?" Likewise, when Noah was made right by his Lord, he too was given a job to do. Noah's job was enormous, costly, time-consuming, and difficult. But it had eternal and global significance. God has a life's work for each of us as well.

Noah Was a Preacher

We are told that Noah was a "preacher of righteousness." Read these words of Peter.

"For if God did not spare angels when they sinned, but cast them into hell and committed them to pits of darkness, reserved for judgment; and did not spare the ancient world, but preserved Noah, a preacher of righteousness, with seven others, when He brought a flood upon the world of the ungodly" (2 Peter 2:4–5)

Noah was building his ship by day and preaching his sermons by night. While he constructed the ark, he instructed people as to the judgment of God. For 120 years he worked doubly hard to proclaim God's grace as he prepared the ark of safety. I have empathy for such a preacher.

Noah prayed, witnessed, shared, testified, and sought to persuade men. Perhaps he went from hut to hut, house to house, family to family, sharing with all who would listen that God was outraged by their sin and that judgment was on its way. His audiences were as cynical as many in our day.

Noah preached for a long time and finally for the last time. Not a single person outside of his family paid the slightest attention to what he said. Perhaps we preachers need to be reminded that we are not responsible for the results, only that we be faithful.

Roger D. Mardis

Noah Was a Leader

Noah preached for more than a century and gained only a handful of converts. I once commented that Noah probably didn't lead his local church association in baptisms, but come to think of it, I guess he did! Noah led first and foremost where it really mattered: at home. He led his family to the Lord and to the ark, and these people were all brought safely through.

From his story, we can easily see that Noah was a believer, a worker, a preacher, and a leader. I hope we are the same.

As today's big door swings closed, let me suggest three things:

(1.) As it was for those in Noah's day, it is true for all of us. Time as we know it will one day end. We don't know when our days will be over, but the Bible says, "It has been appointed unto man once to die and after that the judgment" (Hebrews 9:27). All that will matter is that we are in the ark of God's salvation.
(2.) It is possible to make a difference in our world despite the bad times in which we live. Noah left his mark. A single man made a significant contribution.
(3.) We may not touch hundreds or thousands for our Lord, but we must make sure that we reach our own families.

Many a door seems massive and majestic, but never forget that it swings on small hinges.

But Noah.

Assisi, Italy

But Lot

Genesis 19:6

Yesterday we were introduced to Noah. He could aptly be described as faithful. Today we will meet Lot. He could no doubt be seen as foolish.

As the story unfolds in Genesis, we learn about Lot and his family. In Scripture, we can see what to do from positive examples and what not to do from negative ones. Lot's story is certainly one of those negative examples.

Lot was living it up and he left a wake of destruction. He was more interested in time than in eternity, and his decisions would reflect that. Lot may have had a relationship with the Lord, but he was struggling in his fellowship.

Take time to better acquaint yourself with Lot's story by reading Genesis 13 and 19:1–16, 23–26. There are many lessons to be learned from his life.

His Family

Lot was part of a great family. In fact, his family tree was blessed with some amazing fruit. His uncle Abram, aunt Sarai, and cousin Isaac are all mentioned in Hebrews 11. One day, young Lot followed his godly uncle out of town. They were moving out of Ur of the Chaldees. The people in this special caravan had left not knowing where they would arrive, but they were following the Lord. Abraham "believes God" (Genesis 15:6), and Sarai, Isaac, and Lot all would soon follow suit.

His Faith

Lot was no doubt influenced by godly Abraham, but just because others in our family know the Lord doesn't mean we do too. Salvation's decision is powerful but it's also personal. Lot had to make his own decision.

I've often wondered how that happened. Maybe one day Abraham was preaching. He had pitched his tent, built an altar, and he was exhorting others to come to the Lord. That night young Lot stepped forward, giving his hand to Abraham and his heart to the Lord God.

Granted we don't know how it happened, but we do read in 2 Peter 2:7–8 that Lot was called "that righteous man."

His Foolishness

Lot came to know the Lord, but his life nevertheless went downhill. His relationship with God and men was not right. His heart was separated from God, and he was about to be separated from Abraham. This led Lot to one of those crucial decisions in life. It is certainly true that we make our decisions and then our decisions make us.

Notice how it happened: he saw, he desired, he chose (Genesis 13:10–11). Once Lot made his choice, his life began to spiral out of control. He fell far and fast. First, he pitched his tent toward Sodom (13:12). It was a poor choice. Sodom was a great place to raise cattle but not children. His decision speaks to me of those "borderline" sins. It was a step in the wrong direction. Have you ever taken one of those steps?

Second, he dwelt in Sodom (14:12). Now what in the world was a godly, righteous man like Lot doing in a place like Sodom? Third, he sat in the gate (19:1). Lot had gone from being a journeyman to being a councilman.

This negative movement reminds me of passages in the New Testament. James said we become friends of the world (4:4), John said we begin to love the world (1 John 2:15), and Paul said we end up conformed to the world (Romans 12:1–2). We veer off the proper course in life, become vulnerable, and end up as victims.

Lot was in Sodom, and now Sodom was in Lot. Then we finally read in 19:7, "But Lot." Here was a righteous man, living in a pagan city, making unbelievably poor decisions. In the downward spiral of his life, he had lost his wife, his family, his convictions, and his testimony.

The story has many other themes:

- The utter depravity of the human heart (Jeremiah 17:9).
- God takes sin seriously. If you don't think so, look at the flood, Sodom and Gomorrah, and Mount Calvary.
- When we lose our testimony, our effectiveness and our influence are diminished (Genesis 19:14).
- The ways of this world have a strong grip on a man's life (Genesis 19:16).
- The effects of our poor choices and our sins always linger. It is one thing to get people out of Sodom, but quite another to get Sodom out of people (Genesis 19:30–32).

For Lot, the trouble began with a poor choice and a step in the wrong direction.

But Lot.

Florence, Italy

But the Men

Numbers 13:31

When we speak of change, the conjunction *but* is often attached to a single person, as with those we have already read about. But there are times when it applies to a group of people who alter their course in a positive or negative way. This is true in government. Think of the Congress or the Supreme Court. On a small scale, this may be true of a town council or a school board.

The same type of change may happen in a business, on a team, or in a church. This was the case with a group of God's people, the children of Israel, in their moment of unbelief at Kadesh-Barnea.

Kadesh-Barnea was located on the border of Canaan, the land of promise. Unbelief led Israel to miss God's will and plan. If these people were not careful, they risked spending the rest of their lives wandering aimlessly, just waiting to die.

Surely the story is familiar to us all. The people of God had left Egypt and were on their way to God's Promised Land. However, before they got there they would have to make some crucial choices. Reacquaint yourself with the story in Numbers 13–14.

The story is like a play unfolding before our eyes. There are at least four scenes worth noting. This same play has often been performed by individuals, families, businesses, and churches.

Their Rebellion

I think I have pastored these people before! We preachers often remark that the Scripture shows they are Baptist. Why? They formed a committee. A committee has been called a group of people who individually can do nothing and who collectively decide nothing can be done. I am thankful that when God decided to save the world He didn't form a committee but sent His Son!

Don't be confused by what was happening here. At first glance it appears that God may have been behind this idea, but He wasn't. Read Deuteronomy 1:20–22:

"I said to you, 'You have come to the hill country of the Amorites which the Lord our God is about to give us. See, the Lord your God has placed the land before you; go up, take possession, as the Lord, the God of your fathers, has spoken to you. Do not fear or be dismayed.' Then all of you approached me and said, 'Let us send men before us, that they may search out the land for us, and bring back to us word of the way by which we should go up and the cities which we shall enter.'"

God had said, "Go take the land," but the people reacted with unbelief and fear. They rebelled.

There are times when God allows us to get what we choose, not necessarily what He wants. (He acquiesced again when the Israelites demanded a king named Saul.) God permits these situations to teach His people valuable lessons.

Their Report

The committee had been formed, and now members held a "conference." This involved a thorough expedition that covered some five hundred miles in forty days—and not in a travel trailer! They saw much but learned nothing beyond what God had already told them.

From a human standpoint, one has to appreciate their exhaustive search and their inquisitiveness. What was the land like? What sort of people were there? Were the cities worth inhabiting? What were the opportunities in this land? Their reaction reminds me of the questions that a pastor search committee from another state might ask.

The report had two sides to it. One side was negative. "Giants are there. We can't conquer them. God wouldn't want us to face that." Ten members of the committee agreed with this report. But the majority is not always right. An 83 percent vote is not bad, except when God is on the other side!

There was a positive side. The land was beautiful, fruitful, and productive. The opportunities were off the charts. Thank God for the Joshuas and Calebs of this world. We name our children for them, but no one reading this chapter can name one of the other ten members of the committee.

Their Refusal

God had already promised the people this land. He was simply saying, "Go take it." But the men?

I can hear them now, can't you? "We can't do this. There is no way. We will fail. Look at us compared with them. We are like grasshoppers and they are giants."

Note the New Testament commentary on this story.

> For I do not want you to be unaware, brethren, that our fathers were all under the cloud and all passed through the sea; and all were baptized into Moses in the cloud and in the sea; and all ate the same spiritual food; and all drank the same spiritual drink, for they were drinking from a spiritual rock which followed them; and the rock was Christ. Nevertheless, with most of them God was not well pleased; for they were laid low in the wilderness. Now these things happened as examples for us, so that we would not crave evil things as they also craved. Do not be idolaters, as some of them were; as it is written, "The people sat down to eat and drink, and stood up to play." Nor let

us act immorally, as some of them did, and twenty-three thousand fell in one day. Nor let us try the Lord, as some of them did, and were destroyed by the serpents. Nor grumble, as some of them did, and were destroyed by the destroyer. Now these things happened to them as an example, and they were written for our instruction, upon whom the ends of the ages have come. Therefore let him who thinks he stands take heed that he does not fall. (1 Corinthians 10:1–12)

"And with whom was He angry for forty years? Was it not with those who sinned, whose bodies fell in the wilderness? And to whom did He swear that they would not enter His rest, but to those who were disobedient? So we see that they were not able to enter because of unbelief" (Hebrews 3:17–19).

The writer said that this happened as an example for us. We must learn; we must decide; we must obey God's will and trust His plans. Will we react in fear or respond in faith? Warren Wiersbe once said, "Faith is knowing what God wants you to do and doing it in spite of the concerns within you, the conditions around you or the consequences ahead of you." If the people of Israel had known this, they would have been spared much hardship.

Their Result

Numbers 14 is a picture of what happens when we disobey God's will and disregard what He has said. As you read the chapter, you'll notice division, destruction, and death. Those same results have come to many individuals, families, and churches that disobey God's plan.

What do this story and this hinge "but the men" teach us? What should we glean from these words?

First, God's commandments contain His enablements. Where He directs, He protects. Where He leads, He feeds. Where He guides, He provides.

Second, the majority opinion is not necessarily the right one. God's will is enough.

Third, our unbelief is a serious sin against God; rebellion is like witchcraft (Numbers 13:28–29, 14:11, 22).

Fourth, there comes a time when God's patience wears thin and judgment must come (Numbers 14:18, 23, 28–29, 32, 34).

Fifth, disobedience, even among God's chosen people, may eventually bring God's outright opposition (Numbers 13:34).

Are you today at a Kadesh-Barnea moment in your life? Do you find yourself on the horns of a dilemma? If so, be sure your reaction is one of faith and not of fear. Don't wander the rest of your life just waiting to die. Obey God's will and enjoy His blessings.

But the men.

Dublin, Ireland

But David: Part 1

1 Samuel 17

The story in 1 Samuel 17 is familiar to almost everyone. Surely all churchgoing, Christ-following, Bible-believing people know it. So do many unchurched, unsaved, and unbelieving people. In the world of sports, we often refer to a game or a match as a David vs. Goliath moment. The part the world may not realize is that the big guy loses.

We can all remember a few giants. Stories like *Jack and the Beanstalk* and *Gulliver's Travels* tell us of giants. A program called *Land of the Giants* ran on television for years. When I was young, the wrestling crowd had Andre the Giant. (That was back when wresting was real!) Today we have two professional sporting teams called the Giants.

The Bible introduces us to a giant almost ten feet tall. He was big, bad, and I'm sure quite ugly. David, the shepherd boy, was about to take this giant head on, and then he would take his head off! Read David's story in 1 Samuel 17.

Like David, each of us faces a giant. In fact, we may confront several. Our giants come in different sizes with different strategies and different strengths. But rest assured, they will come.

In 1 Samuel 17, we find that interesting and important word *but* attached to David no less than seven times. Take note of them in verses 15, 24, 29, 34, 45, 50, and 54.

Our Fears

Due to Goliath's size, Saul and his army were living in fear. Goliath reminds us of our own giants. They are powerful. His weapons, armor, and remarks would have intimidated the best of them. They are personal (v. 8). Goliath presented a challenge: find your best man and send him out to me. They are persistent. Giants do not give up, give in, or quit easily. So Goliath was back twice a day for forty days. Giants are paralyzing. They seem to have a spear of fear and their victims are rendered immobile and ineffective. Saul and the others did nothing but live in fear.

Our giants seem to employ the same strategy. They are powerful, personal, persistent, and paralyzing. And we dwell in a spirit of fear.

Our Foes

Are you battling a few giants of your own? Your giant may not be as big as Goliath, but it is as bad. Does your giant have you in the grip of grief or at the tip of his spear of fear?

Your giant may be jealousy. Your giant may be greed. Your giant may be lust. Your giant may be prejudice. Your giant may be an addiction.

Author and pastor Max Lucado writes, "Your giant doesn't carry a sword or a shield. He brandishes blades of unemployment, abandonment, sexual abuse, or depression. Your giant doesn't parade up and down the hills of Elah; he prances through your office, your bedroom, or your classroom. He brings bills you can't pay, grades you can't make, people you can't please, whiskey you can't resist, pornography you can't refuse, a career you can't escape, a past you can't shake, and a future you can't face. You know quite well the roar of your Goliath."

We must all decide, will it be victory or defeat? Will we win or lose? Will we tower over our foes or have them stand over us?

Our Faith

We would all do well to learn from David's example. Notice what he said in 1 Samuel 17:34–36.

"But David said to Saul, 'Your servant was tending his father's sheep. When a lion or a bear came and took a lamb from the flock, I went out after him and attacked him, and rescued it from his mouth; and when he rose up against me, I seized him by his beard and struck him and killed him. Your servant has killed both the lion and the bear; and this uncircumcised Philistine will be like one of them, since he has taunted the armies of the living God.'"

These verses show that David had a past with the Lord. He had seen God come through before, so he knew He would again. Past encounters prepare us for present ones. Little battles prepare us for bigger ones. And private successes prepare us for public ones.

David heard Goliath's roar but he also knew what Saul had said. If he took out Goliath, he could get a wife, great wealth, and a life of true welfare (blessing). How was David's faith evident?

- He trusted the Lord (v. 37).
- He refused Saul's armor (vv. 38–39).
- He gathered his stones (v. 40).
- He ran toward his foe (v. 48).

Where Saul had fled in fear, David walked in faith. Saul and others thought Goliath was too big to hit. David thought he was too big to miss. Saul and others said Goliath was bigger than they were. David knew he was smaller than God. David approached Goliath in the same way we must confront our giants. "You come to me with a sword, spear, and javelin, but I come to you in the name of the Lord of hosts" (v. 45).

- He encouraged others by his own faithfulness (v. 52).
- He celebrated the outcome (v. 54).

Roger D. Mardis

David took Goliath's weapons—a sword, a spear, and a javelin—back to his tent. I wonder if they wound up next to a lion's tail or a bear rug. Each of these items, and perhaps others, stood as a reminder of the faithfulness of David's God.

Whatever the giants or foes you may be facing, load your sling and take your swing. If you approach the giant head on, you can take its head off!

This story, not a fable or a fairy tale, turned on the hinge of that small word *but.*

But David.

Assisi, Italy

But David: Part 2

2 Samuel 11

David had two defining encounters in his life—one with Goliath and the other with Bathsheba. Goliath was his tallest problem, but Bathsheba was his toughest. Goliath was a victory, Bathsheba a defeat. Goliath was a beast; he was big, bad, and ugly. Bathsheba was a beauty; she was soft, gorgeous, and naked.

As a boy, David could tame the lions, but as a man he couldn't conquer his lusts. When he slew Goliath, he provided a morale booster. When he succumbed to temptation, he was guilty of a moral failure.

Read 2 Samuel 11 and be reminded of this sinful saga.

Some suggest that David was about fifty at this time and had perhaps been on the throne for twenty years.

God had told his king not to have multiple wives because this would turn his heart away from the Lord. But David didn't listen to God's command. In fact, he took numerous wives and concubines (2 Samuel 5:13).

Remember that there had been some icy moments at home. David and Michal had a spat (2 Samuel 6). She was the jealous type, and as a royal child, she was accustomed to much dignity. After David returned to Jerusalem with the Ark of the Covenant, she blasted him. His actions humiliated her, and her reaction hurt him. As a result, Michal became barren and David became bored.

Michal disappeared with the other hens fussing about their roosters, and David was lonely. He appeared to be fighting a midlife crisis, and his heart, already dragged away, was now divided.

But David stayed in Jerusalem.

Complacency

The text says it was springtime, which meant wartime. David knew exactly where he was and where he was supposed to be. David was upset, lonely, frustrated, and no doubt discouraged. "Let someone else go to battle," he may have said. "I've fought my fights. I've conquered my giants. I've won my wars."

David had gotten comfortable, and now he was complacent and careless. He had time on his hands, love on his mind, and a wife off the scene. This was a recipe for disaster!

Lust

David's heart was restless and he couldn't sleep. What was a man like David to do? He couldn't turn on *SportsCenter* or watch Andy Griffith reruns. So he got up and walked out onto his roof. From high above, David looked out over his kingdom, his domain, his city. It was late and it was quiet. Finally David heard the splash of water and saw a woman bathing.

The Holy Spirit doesn't use words at random or needlessly, and the text says "the woman was very beautiful." All at once a dagger went from David's eyeballs to his heart. His look became lust, his desire became a decision, his choice became a chain. David had lingered on the roof too long!

Adultery

David saw, he desired, he sent for (2 Samuel 11:2–4). Shakespeare has Caesar making this famous declaration: "Veni, vidi, vici"—"I came, I saw, I conquered." David had his own Shakespearean moment: I saw, I wanted, I took.

Let's keep in mind some worthwhile Bible texts:

"You shall not commit adultery" (Exodus 20:14).

"Marriage is to be held in honor among all, and the marriage bed is to be undefiled; for fornicators and adulterers God will judge" (Hebrews 13:4).

"For the lips of an adulteress drip honey and smoother than oil is her speech; but in the end she is bitter as wormwood, sharp as a two-edged sword" (Proverbs 5:3–4).

"For on account of a harlot one is reduced to a loaf of bread, and an adulteress hunts for the precious life" (Proverbs 6:26).

"The one who commits adultery with a woman is lacking sense; he who would destroy himself does it" (Proverbs 6:32).

At the risk of sounding a little old-fashioned, here is my advice for you gentlemen (and ladies): run, flee, abstain, don't! Don't watch that show. Don't read that magazine. Don't visit that website. Don't respond to that e-mail. Don't listen to those flowery words or that flattering speech. It may appear sweet at the moment, but your mouth will soon be filled with gravel.

You know the outcome. Bathsheba told David she was pregnant, and he went into full-blown cover-up mode. As events transpire, we learn that Uriah had more character drunk than David did sober. So David had to get Uriah out of the picture. In a few days, David had gone from hot-blooded passion to cold-blooded murder. But at least now Uriah was gone and nobody knew the ugly truth.

Oh, really?

David was soon to hear a knock on the door from a preacher, and it was a pastoral visit the king would never forget.

If you are playing with fire, you are going to get burned. If you are entertaining the sins of the flesh, you are living on borrowed time, and they will catch up to you. You too will hear the knock on your door.

But David.

Rome, Italy

But Solomon

1 Kings 11:1–4

As I pen these words, our nation is on the brink of falling over the fiscal cliff. We have dodged and disregarded this crisis for way too long. It seems everyone in Washington has an opinion about what needs to be done to avoid such a disaster, but our nation's elected leaders can't seem to get on the same page.

Big events, big outcomes, and big disasters can all hinge on that little word *but*.

Another leading government official years ago faced a similar impasse. His wasn't a fiscal issue. He did pretty well in that area. His was a physical issue—and a moral one.

Solomon was David's son and the king of Israel. Much of what Solomon did was good and godly. Many of his traits provide worthwhile examples. But they are not the whole story.

You can read about Solomon and his reign in 1 Kings 3–11. What might we learn from this king?

He Trusts the Lord

In many ways, Solomon was a dedicated and dependable man. In fact, he was remarkable, every mother's dream.

We can see several major facets to Solomon's life.

His walk: When he obeyed the Law, he was exemplary. His father had given him a "charge" in 1 Kings 2:3–4, and Solomon sought to make his dad proud. We read in 1 Kings 9:3–5 that he was a man of prayer and integrity.

His wealth (1 Kings 3:13, 10:14–29): God had blessed him with riches and honor. His wealth would make the Buffetts and the Trumps of the world take notice.

His wisdom (1 Kings 3:7–12, 4:29–32, 10:1–3): God had written Solomon a blank check, saying, "Ask whatever you wish." And Solomon knew he needed wisdom, a discerning heart.

His work: Scripture points out Solomon's many accomplishments: the temple, his own house, and so much more.

Here is a summary of his reign.

"So King Solomon became greater than all the kings of the earth in riches and in wisdom. All the earth was seeking the presence of Solomon, to hear his wisdom, which God had put in his heart. They brought every man his gift, articles of silver and gold, garments, weapons, spices, horses, and mules, so much year by year" (1 Kings 10:23–25).

Solomon appeared to be the total package, and he trusted in the Lord. But …

He Turned from the Lord

God had told Solomon (and others) not to marry foreign women, for they would turn his heart away from the Lord. The king ignored this admonition, and the Lord's warning proved right. Solomon's life, once so remarkable, was now deteriorating. Perhaps this change didn't come all at once and Solomon did a slow fade. I once heard it said that we don't fall into sin; we slide into it.

Solomon's heart indeed turned from the Lord. His spiritual life, once vital and strong, was now stagnant. He wasn't spending time with the Lord, his fellowship was suffering, and his discipleship was on a detour. Sound familiar?

God had laid down His law.

"Now the Lord was angry with Solomon because his heart was turned away from the Lord, the God of Israel, who had appeared to him twice, and had commanded him concerning this thing, that he should not go after other gods; but he did not observe what the Lord had commanded" (1 Kings 11:9–10).

But what was Solomon's response? Refusal and rebellion. "This is my life and I'll do with it what I please," he said in effect. Ring any bells?

Every day I hear or read about someone yielding to the temptation and pressures of sin. The choice may have happened in a moment, but the groundwork was laid over time. The person fell after turning away from the things of the Lord.

Solomon started strong, but he loved many foreign women, and they led him to false gods.

He Speaks for the Lord

Solomon was the human author of three books of the Bible: Proverbs, Ecclesiastes, and the Song of Solomon. They are books of rules (Proverbs), romance (Song of Solomon), and regrets (Ecclesiastes). It's been suggested that he wrote the Song of Solomon when he was young, in love, and in the prime of life; that he wrote Proverbs in middle age when he was a seasoned man with much wisdom to offer, and that he wrote Ecclesiastes as an old man, living a life of regret. He looked back over his wasted life and all he could say was "vanity."

If only Solomon had lived out the proverbs he wrote.

Do you want the story of your life to resemble the Song of Solomon or Ecclesiastes? You must make a choice between victory or vanity.

Solomon's experience is being played out in the lives of people just like you every day. Stoke the fire of your heart, walk, and marriage so you don't grow cold, carnal, and complacent.

But Solomon.

Prague, Czech Republic

But Uzziah

2 Chronicles 26:1–23

Today we will look at the young king Uzziah, who dealt with an age-old problem: pride.

Uzziah was only sixteen when the people rebelled and killed his father, Amaziah. He succeeded him as king of Judah. Uzziah is an abbreviated name for Azariah.

This boy king was sincere and successful. However, Uzziah became prideful, arrogant, and impressed with his own press clippings. He was removed from the throne as an older man.

I've met people like him, and I'm sure you have as well. They are full of themselves, and they want you to know just how important they are. They may lead a big business, a big church, or a big life. Talk about strutting—they can do it sitting down!

That's the kind of person Uzziah became, and it cost him dearly. In one short chapter, he went from a lad to a leader to a leper. But Uzziah! Read his story in 2 Chronicles 26:1–23.

His Ascension to the Throne

Uzziah was only a teenager when he took the throne. While his peers were trying to secure their chariot licenses or make the travel squad for the Canaan Camels, Uzziah was being crowned king.

Can you imagine the conversation on the following Monday? "Hey, Uz, what did you do this weekend?" "Well, I became king, and the name is not Uz—it is King Uzziah!"

His Accomplishments as King

The names Uzziah and Azariah are important. Uzziah means "God is mighty," and Azariah means "God helps or God is my help." This mighty God was obviously helping the naïve king. Reading chapter 26, you will see that he chalked up several great accomplishments with the help of his God.

- He built great ports in strategic cities like Eloth (v.2).
- He defeated the Philistines (vv. 6–7). It's always good to get a few victories under your belt!
- He built great cities and strong military outposts (v. 6).
- He fortified the walls of Jerusalem and built towers for lookouts (v. 9).
- He dug many cisterns in the wilderness to preserve the lives of the people and livestock (v. 10).
- He armed his soldiers with the best equipment (vv. 11–15).
- He built a powerful and elite army (v. 13).

During Uzziah's early days, the kingdom grew. Materially and militarily, all was good for Judah. Young Uzziah was a difference maker. Verse 8 says, "He became very strong."

Abominations That Cost Him the Throne

King Uzziah went up like a rocket but came down like a rock. Speaking about young preachers with little experience filling pulpits in influential churches, Adrian Rogers once remarked, "You can get there too fast." We all know where "there" is, and Uzziah was "there."

Uzziah made a series of poor choices.

- He acted corruptly (v. 16).
- He was unfaithful to the Lord (v. 16).
- He thought he was above the Law (vv. 16–20).
- He resented the warnings of others (vv. 17–19).

As a result, God smote him with leprosy (v. 19). Uzziah lived as a leper until his death. This meant being separated from everyone else (v. 21).

Many preachers, executives, and other leaders have done the same thing. They have forgotten who they are, where they came from, and who put them where they are. They have lived large and loose. They have become unteachable and unapproachable.

They may not have leprosy, but they are just as defiled and dirty. They too have forfeited their right to lead.

Some Applications We Can Make

Pride is one of the leading weapons in the devil's arsenal. When we start thinking we are hot stuff and demand attention for ourselves, we can be sure we are about to lose the crowns we've placed on our heads.

"Pride goes before destruction, and a haughty spirit before stumbling" (Proverbs 16:18).

"A man's pride will bring him low, but a humble spirit will obtain honor" (Proverbs 29:23).

The word *pride* is not so big, and neither is the person struck by it! Right in the middle of this word is *I*. That will get us in trouble every time.

If pride will make a devil out of an angel and a leper out of a king, what might it do to us? Pride makes us feel as if we don't need God, His love, His salvation, or His commands. Pride is at the core of every sin we commit.

It has been well said that pride is the only disease known to man that makes everyone sick except the person who has it. Nothing is more distasteful to God than self-conceit.

But Uzziah.

Location Unknown

But Daniel

Daniel 1:8

Several years ago the name Cassie Bernall became widely known. Up until that fateful day at Columbine High School in Littleton, Colorado, not many people had heard of this sweet, young Christian girl. But on this day all of that changed.

Two male gunmen walked into Cassie's high school with assault weapons and ample ammunition. Their targets were said to be Christian students. One of them was Cassie. She, along with eleven other students and one teacher, lost her life that day.

Much has been written about Cassie and the others. The bottom line is that she was one tough teen, and the courageous way she faced death has affected thousands of people.

The prophet Daniel was also a tenacious teen at one time. He was brought up in a good way and at a good time. Josiah's reign had brought revival and reformation, but something was about to change for young Daniel and his friends. Read the story in Daniel 1:1–8.

Daniel Was a Fine "Moral Man"

Daniel and his friends have been taken to Babylon and enrolled in the University of Paganism. These young men would have ample opportunity to defile themselves.

A similar thing happens to teens who go off to college and begin to know a newfound "liberty." They are away from their parents, their pastors, and many of their peers, and they face many new decisions.

Daniel was in a new land (v. 3) with unfamiliar scenery. He was reading a new literature (v. 4). The system wants young people to think differently, so it reprograms their minds, often turning their thoughts the wrong way. It's okay for our minds to be challenged, but they shouldn't be corrupted.

They were taught a new language (v. 4). We want our teens to think and to talk differently. Those boys were taken out of their comfort zones and placed in the midst of corruption. They were instructed to live a new lifestyle (v. 5), to eat and to drink what the Babylonians did. Their masters wanted to control how the boys lived. They were given new loyalties (vv. 6–7). I know that because their names were changed.

Daniel means "God is my judge," but Beltshazzar declares, "Baal protect my life." Hahaniah means "the Lord shows grace," but Shadrach means "the command of Aku." Mishael means "who is like God," but Meshach means "who is as Aku is." Azariah declares, "The Lord is my helper," but Abed-nego means "the servant of Nebo." Each of these new names referred to a pagan deity and was intended to establish new loyalties.

King Nebuchadnezzar was seeking to corrupt Daniel and his friends. He wanted to conform them, transform them, and deform them. But as tough as their environment was, these boys were up to the task.

Daniel Made a Series of Wise Decisions

Daniel and his friends were among the elite young men of their day. They were people of ability, strength, and knowledge, and they were handsome. There was no defect in their character. But they were put to a test and had to make a decision.

Some of the things happening around Daniel and his friends he could control and others he couldn't. But being in a new land, reading new literature, and learning a new language would not automatically make the boys submit. When it came to their food, Daniel and the others drew a line in the sand. The food they were told to eat was going to make them unclean. These Jewish boys would eat only what God had approved.

This same thing happens on college campuses every year. There are situations that students cannot control. This is true in many state schools and even in some Christian-based institutions. But when it comes to character issues such as cheating, drinking, drug use, theft, and bad movies or music, students must make godly decisions.

Daniel made such a decision. It came from the heart. Solomon said, "Watch over your heart with all diligence, for from it flows the springs of life" (Proverbs 4:23). We must all do this and teach our teens to follow suit. We make our decisions, and then our decisions will make us.

God Honored Daniel's Life and Decisions

The good news is that just as God honored Daniel's life, He will honor ours. God blessed his decisions, and He will bless ours. It doesn't take much backbone to go with the flow and be part of the crowd, but it takes guts to say no and to be different. We should challenge our young people to dare to be different, to dare to be Daniels.

We lose every time we compromise. Adam and Eve compromised and lost paradise. Abraham compromised and almost lost his wife. Sarah compromised, and because of Hagar and Ishmael, we lost peace in the Middle East. Esau compromised and lost his birthright. Moses compromised and lost his chance to enter the Promised Land. David compromised and lost his child. Ananias and Sapphira compromised and lost their lives. Judas compromised and lost his soul.

Our culture's message seems to be that if you want to get ahead, you've got to break a few rules along the way, to lie a little, cheat a little, compromise your morals and values. But God honored the life of Daniel and the choices he made.

That choice had an impact on him. He had intelligence and was given insight. In the process, Daniel and his friends influenced many others. He eventually became the kingdom's prime minister. God preserved him and protected him and finally promoted him.

Throughout this ordeal, God was present, just as He is during your trials, tests, temptations, and tragedies. If Daniel had done what Ashphenaz told him to do, he would not be in the Hall of Faith, but in the Room of Failure. Everything hinges on that small word *but*. "But Daniel purposed in his heart."

Young reader or older parent, don't give up and don't give in. Stay focused in your life of faith and become an obedient follower of our Lord Jesus.

Be a Daniel or maybe even a Cassie Bernall. Make wise, godly decisions, and let God do with your life as He has purposed.

But Daniel.

Assisi, Italy

But Jonah: Part 1

Jonah 1:1–3

We all have a little bit of Jonah in us. How is that so? You may ask. Have you ever refused to do something you knew God wanted you to do? Maybe it was to teach a class, go back to school, enter the ministry, make a visit, or go on a mission trip. God spoke so clearly to your heart that you knew His will, but you simply wouldn't obey.

All of us may have been guilty of this at one time or another. Jonah certainly was.

We have all seen believers struggle in their walk, rebel against the Lord's will, or abandon God altogether. But when a preacher does it, there is a greater sense of disappointment. It happened to Simon Peter. It happened to Jim Bakker. It happened to Bob Harrington. It also happened to Jonah.

Jonah the Messenger

Jonah was God's man, His chosen servant, and He had called Jonah to take His message of repentance and forgiveness to the people of Ninevah. The Ninevites were a wicked and rebellious people. They were hateful and mean. Jonah was not terribly excited about God's revelation. He knew about these people. Jonah didn't want to go. He didn't want to obey. In fact, Jonah didn't want them changed—he wanted them judged!

Before we come down too hard on Jonah, what would your response be if God sent you or one of your loved ones to such a place?

Maybe the people there would be of a different color or their culture would be challenging. Maybe they wouldn't look like us or talk like us or worship like us.

In most Bible translations the book of Jonah begins with the word *and*. This book is one of fourteen in the Bible that begin this way. These books and the word remind us that God's Word is one big story of grace and mercy. There are sixty-six books in the Scripture, but only one story. That story is God's plan to seek and save lost sinners.

God told Jonah where to go, what to do, and why He wanted him to go. It was a simple message, one Jonah should have obeyed. But Jonah, instead of trusting God and following His call, sought to get as far away from the Lord as possible.

Why didn't Jonah go? Maybe for the same reason some of us don't obey the Lord: fear. Nineveh was a large city with perhaps a million inhabitants. It was the capital city of Assyria, and it was a mean and wicked place. Historians tell us of the Ninevites' many heinous and cruel crimes against humanity. They would bury people alive, skin them alive, and string them up between poles and rip off their limbs. They would impale people on sharp poles in the hot sun and boil others to death in pots of oil.

Fear has a way of paralyzing us too. Jonah wasn't exited about such a calling, and we might not have been either.

Maybe he was prejudiced. Perhaps this Jewish man didn't want to preach to a Gentile audience. "I'll go to my kind of people," he may have said. Perhaps Jonah simply lacked compassion. He didn't love the Ninevites enough, or he didn't love them at all! He didn't care about their souls or about where they would spend eternity. "Why do I have to be the one to go there?" he might have asked.

Maybe the problem was Jonah's awareness. He knew what God would do. He knew God was merciful and gracious. He knew that if the Ninevites repented God would forgive them. So what did Jonah do instead?

He Rebelled

Jonah went to Tarshish, not to Nineveh. On your Bible map, you'll find Tarshish (Tartessus) on the southern tip of Spain. It was in exactly the opposite direction from Nineveh.

I live in Alabama. If God called me to go to Tennessee, I would have to travel north. If I went to Florida, I would go south. I would be doing just the opposite of what God told me to do. When Jonah boarded that boat to Tarshish, that's what he was doing.

He Ran

Jonah was on the run. Can you imagine trying to get away from God? Tarshish was the farthest known distance from Palestine by sea. Jonah wanted to get as far away from God as he could.

Do you have a Tarshish in your life? Have you conveniently boarded a wrong ship? Satan will make your rebellion seem almost providential. *What a divine appointment*, you may think, when deep down you know you're living in rebellion and you're running as fast as you can in the opposite direction from where God wants you to be. Disobedience can at times be so convenient.

He Regretted

Running from God is foolish. Jonah tried and so have many other people, but he wasn't successful and you won't be either. Resisting God's will is always costly (v. 3). If you go with God He pays the fare, but when you rebel, you pay—dearly. Rebellion is also dangerous. As you read this story, it's hard to miss the storm, the sea, and the upset sailors!

It's impossible for one of God's children to flee Him. When you try to run from God, you'll run right into Him. Read the words of the psalmist.

"Where can I go from Your Spirit? Or where can I flee from Your presence? If I ascend to heaven, You are there; if I make my bed in Sheol, behold, You are there. If I take the wings of the dawn, if I dwell in the remotest part of the sea, even there Your hand will lead me, and Your right hand will lay hold of me" (Psalm 139:7–10).

Thankfully, we know the rest of Jonah's story. The question is, do you know the rest of yours? Are you living in rebellion and running from the will of God? Doing this will lead only to regret until you make it right. Don't end up in the belly of a big fish. Reverse your course today.

But Jonah.

Annapolis, Maryland

But Jonah: Part 2

Jonah 4:1

We saw yesterday that all of us have a little Jonah in us. Jonah went from praying to preaching to pouting.

In chapter 2, we see that Jonah prayed. In fact, he prayed quite a prayer, and why not? It has been said that it's easy to pray in times of desperation. And being in the belly of a big fish, sinking to the bottom of the sea with no hope of survival, qualifies for desperation! Yet God heard Jonah's prayer. It's interesting to see that in the worst of times Jonah prays the best of prayers, but in the best of times (4:2) he prays the worst of prayers.

In chapter 3, we read that Jonah preached. It wasn't a long or elaborate sermon with three points, timely illustrations, a catchy introduction, or a set-the-hook conclusion. In fact, there were only eight words. (Please don't tell my congregation that!) I must admit there was a really good illustration, and it was the preacher himself. Skin bleached from the gases of the fish's stomach, clothes half digested, he exuded a foul odor as he brushed away the seaweed. The sight of Jonah alone would have made the speech worthwhile! And when he said, "Get right!," his listeners did—all of them.

In chapter 4, we see that Jonah pouted. If only the book had ended at chapter 3, because we read in 4:1, "But ..." Incredibly, what God had done greatly displeased Jonah. The Ninevites got revived but Jonah rebelled. The townspeople got right but the preacher went wrong.

Before we address Jonah's attitude, let's note something of great importance. You see, this book is not about the great fish, a great storm, a great city, or even a great revival; it's about a great God. Despite

Jonah's early rebellion, God's compassion and calling and command to him had not changed.

Maybe you have endured a season of rebellion or have survived some rather trying storms of your own. Remember that God's compassion for you has not changed. He still loves you with an everlasting love. In fact, He still has a job for you to do and a message for you to share. It's time to get to your Nineveh!

The book of Jonah is not a mystical book; it's a missionary one. In it we can see the following:

- There are great needs in faraway places (1:1–2).
- A true missionary focus is fueled by prayer (2:1–2, 4:2).
- While God was working in Jonah and on Jonah, He was also working through him. Revival didn't come because of Jonah, but in spite of him.
- God's love is amazing. He is a missionary God and a merciful one.
- God showed mercy to the people of Nineveh but also to Jonah. Evidently, Jonah got right with the Lord, because we don't read his obituary.

God did an amazing work, provided a miraculous delivery of Jonah, and performed many other miracles of grace and mercy, but Jonah wasn't happy. In fact, he got angry and argued with God. (Okay, call it prayer, but his heart wasn't right!)

Have you ever done this? God performed a mighty deed. His power was displayed and His glory was revealed, but maybe it didn't happen in the way you might have chosen, so you got a little upset, even angry, at Him. Are you kidding me? The words of God to Jonah are worth hearing: "Do you have good reason to be angry?" (4:4)

I learned years ago that when God shows up, He doesn't take orders, He takes over. And He is not obligated to do what I want or to work in ways I choose. We must quit trying to put God in our own little box. He is way too big and He won't fit!

God had to confront and to deal with Jonah's pride and prejudice. He must do the same with ours.

But Jonah.

Florence, Italy

But the Rich Young Ruler

Mark 10:17–22

The passage in question today is one of my favorites. In fact, when I preached my first sermon more than three decades ago, this was the passage I shared. Honestly, it was probably a homiletical disaster, though I don't recall a thing I said. (Maybe the audience doesn't either!)

The rich young ruler approached Jesus as He was teaching. The Lord was discussing divorce, the kingdom, His own suffering, and faith. Jesus was surrounded by children, and He was about to set down rules for entrance into His kingdom. He explained how people of all ages must enter.

The children were dependent on Him. By contrast, the rich young ruler didn't need anyone's assistance, or so he thought.

When you put the three synoptic gospels together, you see the reason for the title "rich young ruler." Matthew says he was a "young man" (19:20) and wealthy. Luke says he was powerful, i.e., a ruler (18:18). Mark suggests he was religious, for he "kept all those things" (10:20).

When the rich young ruler approached Jesus, he asked an interesting question, "What must I do to inherit eternal life?" The Lord's reply was also interesting. We should not suppose that He was making a case for universal asceticism, the idea of giving up all wealth and privilege and conveniences and living a life of complete self-denial. Christ's reply is not to be understood as a mandate for all would-be followers. But it was appropriate in this case. Jesus does demand of all followers that they put away all gods and idols, and that is what riches had become for this man.

Jesus was testing the young man. The exam was based on Christ's words in Luke 14:33, "So then, none of you can be My disciple who does not give up all his own possessions." Would this man trust in his position and his possessions, or would he place his faith in the person of Christ? The rich young ruler's report card was now in, and he had failed this crucial test.

What might we learn from this encounter? Read Mark 10:17–22.

The Rich Young Ruler Coming (v. 17).

The young man came to the one who is life's answer and who could satisfy his deepest longing. He came at the right time. Solomon tells us to remember our creator in the days of our youth (Ecclesiastes 12:1). He came to the right person— the Lord Jesus, the Son of God, the Savior of the World, the One who could give him eternal life. He asked the right question, "What must I do to be saved?" He got the right answer. Jesus told him exactly what he needed to hear, but it wasn't what he wanted to hear.

I have seen that countless times in my years of pastoral ministry. Folks take the time to come see me because they need direction or counsel in an area of life. All goes well until they hear biblical wisdom that is contrary to what they have already decided. Folks, save yourselves and your pastor time and frustration. If you don't want Bible counsel, don't ask a Bible preacher!

So, as with the rich young ruler, in many cases we have the right time, the right person, the right answer, but the wrong response.

The Rich Young Ruler Searching (v. 17)

Evidently his possessions, his position, and his power weren't enough. They didn't satisfy him. He needed eternal life, not temporary leisure. The term *eternal life* is strictly biblical. In fact, it is found almost fifty times in the Scripture. Here are some examples:

"And this is eternal life that they may know you" (John 17:13).

"The gift of God is eternal life" (Romans 6:23).

"And I give unto them eternal life" (John 10:28).

"Whosoever believeth in Him should not perish, but have eternal life" (John 3:16).

So many today are looking for love in all the wrong places.

The Rich Young Ruler Hearing (vv. 18–19)

The Lord was keenly aware of who this man was and what he represented, and he gave him a three-point sermon. It was a sermon first on God. "Why call Me good?" Jesus asked the man. "No one is good but God alone." Jesus was asking, "Do you want Me to be your God?" It was also a sermon on God's law. We call the law the Ten Commandments. The first four deal with our vertical relationship— that is, our relationship with God. The next six involve our horizontal relationships, those with other human beings.

Jesus quoted for the young man commandments five, six, seven, eight, and nine. The command missing was number ten. That was the Lord's point. "Your gods," he was saying, "are wealth and possessions. Stop coveting power, money, and position."

This led to the sermon's third point—God's requirement. Jesus told the man to get rid of his little gods and come to Him. The sermon is still useful today: God, God's law, God's requirement.

The Rich Young Ruler Deciding

The Lord's sermon had been preached, and now it was time for a response. The young man had heard the terms and knew what was necessary, but he chose not to obey. We have decisions every Sunday at our church; not to decide is to decide wrongly.

This man was unwilling to obey and unwilling to believe (i.e., have faith) even though God said he would have treasure in heaven. You and I have seen many folks just like him. They choose wrongly.

The Rich Young Ruler Grieving (v. 22)

Instead of believing God and becoming the recipient of eternal life and treasure in heaven, this guy chose his own kingdom and it would topple. The Scripture says, "His face fell." Matthew 16:3 describes the face of the sky as becoming "red and threatening" with an approaching storm. The rich young ruler had made his decision and he would face the consequences. His life would grow dark with dismay.

This story started out so right, but it went so wrong.

Jesus ended the sermon and provided an interesting illustration for his other listeners when he talked about a camel going through the eye of a needle. I once heard a preacher say, "They either had smaller camels or larger needles." Truth is, camels, cows, coyotes, cats, cardinals, caterpillars—none can go through the eye of a needle.

The Lord was saying, if you trust anything or anyone else to give you eternal life, it won't happen; it's impossible. But if you place your faith in God, all things are possible (Mark 10:27).

So much of the young man's life was admirable, but there was one thing he lacked.

But the rich young ruler.

Washington, D.C.

Proverbial "Buts"

Proverbs (Selected Passages)

A careful study of every Bible book will probably reveal the hinge word *but*. It is found in the books of Moses, of history, of poets, and of prophets, in the gospels, the epistles, and the apocalyptic literature.

However, this hinge word may well occur most often in the book of Proverbs. For years I have tried to read a chapter from this book every day. I'm sure it's more beneficial than my city's paper!

It wasn't until the last few years that I noticed the word *but* in this book.

The writer, Solomon, I believe was on to something. A proverb has been called a short sentence based on long experience. A proverb is brief and pictorial.

It's important to understand that Solomon wrote a book of proverbs, not of promises. It has been said that a proverb is a generalized statement of what is generally true. For example, Proverbs 15:1 says, "A soft answer turns away wrath." Now, that is normally true, but there are times when you can be as sweet as sugar and gentle as a dove and still be cussed out!

Solomon was the human author of three books of Scripture. He penned the Song of Songs (Solomon), Proverbs, and Ecclesiastes. The first is a book of romance, the second a book of rules, and the last a book of regrets. It has been suggested that each book was written at a different point in Solomon's life—in his youth, in middle age, and in his final years.

Proverbs has been likened to a string of pearls. Just as every pearl is beautiful, costly, and treasured, so is every proverb. It's as if Solomon was writing words of wisdom for Rehoboam (and others). Do this; don't do that; learn from my mistakes.

There are several hundred *buts* in this book, so we will not look at them all. I challenge you to mark them all with your pen or your highlighter as you fill your heart with Solomon's wisdom each day. (There are thirty-one chapters. Read them by matching each one to the day of the month. For example, on May 12, read Proverbs 12.)

Solomon offered advice on six ideas or issues.

Sexual Sin (Proverbs 5:1-4)

Indeed, we are living in the midst of a sexual revolution. What once was forbidden, rarely discussed, and seldom printed or filmed is now mainstreamed. Solomon was not immune to sexual sins; nor were his parents. It would not hurt any man, young or old, to meditate regularly on Proverbs 5–9.

I can't begin to tell you the number of horror stories I hear weekly of people's sexual license, perversion, and indiscretions. Learn this: sexual sins promise pleasure but they deliver death.

Loose Lips (Proverbs 10:19)

A careful study of Proverbs reveals that the wise king had much to say about our words, our oaths, and our declarations. Multiple proverbs deal with our words. As children we sang, "O be careful little mouth what you say. O be careful little mouth what you say, for the Father up above is listening down in love. O be careful little mouth what you say."

James likened our words to poison, fire, and a destructive wild beast. It is always wise to think before you speak. Many of the sins God hates most involve our words (Proverbs 6:16–19).

Neglected Notes (Proverbs 11:15)

Solomon uses the word *guarantor*. Here's the idea: don't co-sign on someone else's bank note or pledge. If you do, more times than not, you'll end up paying the note.

A banker friend in my town told me, "Roger, there is a reason the bank asks some customers to get a parent or a friend to co-sign with them. It's because they have bad credit and have been deemed bad risks. We as parents need to teach our children industry, work, and financial integrity, and we shouldn't nullify all these things by co-signing their notes."

Scripture says the borrower becomes the lender's slave. When you co-sign a note or loan money to or borrow from a friend or family member, the relationship is destined to change for the worse.

Worthless Workers (Proverbs 12:11)

We are living in strange days and are seeing things that past generations never imagined. We've become the land of entitlement. Many adults and young people feel they are entitled to a payday, insurance, a cell phone, and whole list of handouts without working. They don't want to get up, leave the cave, kill something, and drag it home. This culture says, "Let me sleep in. You fix my problems, you pay my bills, and you satisfy my needs."

People want something for nothing. This proverb deals with that demand. One of the best things I can do for my family is to model financial integrity and a strong work ethic. My children need to know that manual labor is not the president of a foreign country and that get-rich-quick schemes never work (Proverbs 28:19).

Hidden Habits (Proverbs 28:13)

If we begin to hide our sins instead of dealing with them, trouble is not on the way—it is already here. So many times we become like Achan, possessing (and hiding) things under God's ban.

Solomon reminds us that this is not the type of life God will bless. Rather, to find and to gain God's compassion, we must "confess and forsake" our sins. That is, we must agree with God over the matter and cut the cord with our faulty ways.

Tiny Things (Proverbs 30:24–28)

Life seems to say to us that bigger is better and smaller is insignificant. Solomon could not have disagreed more. In fact, he said that some of the smallest animals on the earth are very wise. Hmm, that's interesting.

He told us to look at and learn from the ant, the badger, the locust, and the lizard. As we study them, we notice how they live, where they live, and the way they maneuver. Solomon said they are wise in their ways.

The world tells us, "Don't sweat the small stuff," but Solomon would counsel to the contrary. You better give attention to detail. Don't overlook the fine print. Continue to do the little things, and do them well consistently.

Solomon was indeed a wise man, and we would do well to read his words and to heed his warnings. We had better sweat the small stuff!

But the Proverbs.

Republic of Malta

But Shadrach, Meshach, and Abed-nego

Daniel 3:1–30

Daniel 3 is one of the most exciting chapters in the Bible. All of us were introduced to it as young children, and the message and the images stuck. As we read about the hostility and hatred of King Nebuchadnezzar and about the heat of Babylon's furnace, we find another door. We see two crucial hinges. They are found in verses 15 and 18.

The Babylonians seemed to be challenging Daniel's convictions and calling into question the courage of his three friends.

So much of life is a test. A faith that cannot be tested can't be trusted! When these tests come our way, they might blow in like a storm, surface by way of some sorrow, or apply the heat like a fiery furnace.

The apostle Peter must have learned this analogy, because he used the metaphor of a fiery ordeal more than once. For example, he said in 1 Peter 1:7, "So that the proof of your faith, being more precious than gold which is perishable, even though tested by fire, may be found to result in praise and glory and honor at the revelation of Jesus Christ." He repeated the idea in 1 Peter 4:12: "Beloved, do not be surprised at the fiery ordeal among you, which comes upon you for your testing, as though some strange thing were happening to you."

In the first three chapters of Daniel, we see this test unfold for the prophet and his friends. In chapter 1 their walk was tested; in chapter 2 their witness was tested; in chapter 3 their worship was tested.

Daniel and those Hebrew boys had great upbringings, godly values, and firm convictions. They knew God's laws and commandments, and He had said they should have no other gods and no idols (Exodus 20:3–4). So they were ushered into the laboratory of life and the time of testing began. Would they bend? Would they bow? Would they budge?

After a momentary look toward God in chapter 2, Nebuchadnezzar had turned from the Lord and abandoned his short-lived (false) faith. He created a statue of gold ninety feet high and nine feet wide. It must have been a sight to see. Then he invited everyone to come and worship this golden idol. Everybody who was somebody attended the unveiling.

I'm sure BNN, the Babylonian News Network, carried the event live. The pressure was as intense as the raging fire in the furnace. Nebuchadnezzar, like Satan, used fear and peer pressure. Everyone was to bow down and worship the image, and everyone did—except the Hebrew boys.

The leaders of Nebuchadnezzar's kingdom came to the king to report the "disobedience" of these three foreigners. At first, the king was as hot as his furnace. Then he calmed down for a moment and gave the boys a second chance. He said, "Is it true, Shadrach, Meshach, and Abed-nego, that you do not serve the golden image I have set up? Now if you are ready, at the moment you hear the music, fall down to worship, and all will be okay. But if you do not, you will be thrown into the fiery furnace."

This furnace was perhaps like a crematorium, resembling a potbellied stove with large openings at the top and the bottom. The victims would have been cast into the top. The king had his stove burning, ready for all those who disobeyed his orders.

Here is where the story gets interesting. These young men didn't need a second chance or time to pray about their responses. Their minds were made up and wouldn't be changed, because they believed God could deliver them. When you face your own fiery ordeals, do you have such confidence? Read their words:

"Shadrach, Meshach and Abed-nego replied to the king, 'O Nebuchadnezzar, we do not need to give you an answer concerning this matter. If it be so, our God whom we serve is able to deliver us from the furnace of blazing fire; and He will deliver us out of your hand, O king. But even if He does not, let it be known to you, O king, that we are not going to serve your gods or worship the golden image that you have set up'" (Daniel 3:16–18).

Much has been said and written on this subject, but let me make two points.

Our God Is Able!

These boys knew the Word of God and the God of the Word. They believed that God was who He said He was and that He could do what He said He could do. It is high time we decide to live with this same confidence.

Do you need grace? God is able! (2 Corinthians 9:8)
Do you need help to overcome some temptation? God is able! (Hebrews 2:18)
Do you need salvation and deliverance? God is able! (Hebrews 7:25)
Do you need security? God is able! (2 Timothy 1:12)
Do you need strength? God is able! (Jude 24–25)
The key is found in Daniel 3:18. These three young men placed their faith and confidence not in what God could do but in who God is.

But Even if He Doesn't …

It is so much easier to serve God, surrender to His plans, and sing His praises when He answers our prayers and does things our way. But what if He doesn't? In those moments, we learn more about us than we do about Him.

While writing this chapter, I got a text message from my brother-in-law saying he had taken my sister to the hospital. She was suffering chest pains, nausea, and dizziness. I told him I would be praying.

I stopped writing to breathe a word of prayer on her behalf. In doing so, I quoted these words: "God, you are able, but even if You do not work in the way I so choose, it will not alter who You are or affect how I feel about You."

Shadrach, Meshach, and Abed-nego believed that God could deliver them, but they were going to trust Him even if He did not. That is how our faith is supposed to operate.

Surely, you know how the story ends and have heard the sermon points. They were bound and cast into the fire. They were joined in the fire by the God they served. They were liberated from their bindings. They were not hurt by the fire, and they didn't even smell like smoke. Now that is a good outcome. I do not care how many times you've read it!

We will learn some lessons only in our furnace experiences. You might be having one now. I believe God will never use us as effectively as He can until we have endured seasons of suffering. The road to glory is paved with difficulty. Along the way, do not bend, bow, or budge and you won't burn!

But Shadrach, Meshach, and Abed-nego.

Assisi, Italy

But the Righteous

Habakkuk 2:4

If you have overlooked the book of Habakkuk, you are penalizing yourself. It is one of the twelve books we call the Minor Prophets section of the Old Testament. Habakkuk is not "minor" because it is less inspired or less inspiring but because it is short. This, however, is a minor prophet with a major message.

In many ways, Habakkuk (the writer) resembles us. He was living in a tough time. The king was Jehoiakim, and he was wicked and his rule was abusive. Jehoiakim distorted and destroyed the words of God.

Habakkuk also had some tough experiences. He embodied the age-old question, why do bad things happen to good people? We might also wonder why the wicked prosper and the righteous suffer.

But reading his words, it's clear that a change was coming over his soul. He went from worry in chapter 1 to worship in chapter 3. In chapter 1 he was in a valley, but in chapter 3 he was on the mountain. Chapter 1 calls for a question mark, but chapter 3 demands an exclamation point. Chapter 1 is full of sorrow, but chapter 3 is a glorious song.

The hinge found in chapter 2 makes all the difference. Take a few moments to read these three chapters. Together there are only fifty-six verses. Concentrate on our key verse, 2:4.

The prophet accused God of being indifferent, inactive, and inconsistent. As you read the first chapter, you hear this man arguing and fussing with God. Can you imagine talking back to the Lord? Now before you get too critical of Habakkuk, don't we do the same thing when we ask God "Why?" or "Where were you?" or even "How long, Lord?"

Habakkuk did a wise thing in chapter 2. He decided to "climb the tower" and get another perspective on what was happening. All of us need a tower, a place where we can be alone with the Lord, take our honest questions to Him, and try to see things from His point of view, not from ours.

We can learn from and apply God's ways (His revelations) by understanding two points. First, God's timing is what counts (2:3). We serve an on-time God who controls circumstances and is not controlled by them. God will deal with all of life's issues and injustices in His way and in His time. Bank on it, my friends.

Second, our faith is essential, as verse 2:4 makes clear. This verse is one of the greatest in the Bible. In fact, it will be repeated three times in the New Testament. Here, however, it compares two groups: Babylonians and believers. The Babylonians have faulty hearts. Their souls are not right within them. But believers have faith-filled hearts, for "the righteous will live by faith."

The key change is found in the word *but*. When we view things through a human lens, we will become skeptical and cynical like the Habakkuk of chapter 1. However, if we view life's happenings through the lens of faith we will learn to trust God's ways.

It is interesting that Habakkuk's words are repeated by the apostle Paul in three New Testament passages (that's if you believe Paul authored the epistle to the Hebrews). Paul pens these words in Romans 1:17, Galatians 3:11, and Hebrews 10:38. Three times he says, "The just shall live by faith."

It has been suggested that Romans illustrates the concept of "the just." This epistle speaks of our being declared righteous by faith in the Lord. Galatians explains how believers "shall live." Here Paul addresses how the faithful walk, live, and serve. Hebrews shows us the meaning of "by faith." We leave life's elementary ways and move on toward a life of faith, trusting the Lord.

Historians remind us that these words were the keys to the Reformation. Martin Luther had become aware of his own sin and of his inability to resolve these issues. He entered the monastery and began to study Paul's letter to the Romans. When he meditated on Romans 1:17—"but the just shall live by faith"— God gripped his heart and the glorious light of grace shone into his soul.

Luther journeyed to Rome and found himself at the judgment hall of Pilot, and here he supposedly "kissed the blood." In this way, he accepted God's claim of salvation by faith alone and was born again. He left the Church of Rome and took half of Europe with him. We call it the Protestant Reformation.

All of this hinged on the little word *but*. Do not view life and its happenings through any lens other than faith in God's perfect Word. It just might bring a revolution!

In this way, you can live life like Habakkuk. By chapter 3 things are dramatically different. What started as a sob is now a song.

What changed? Had God changed? No. Had life's circumstances changed? No. Had Habakkuk changed? Yes. He now trusted the Lord. Even if we can't make heads or tails of our circumstances, we would do well to recall the prophet's words:

"Though the fig tree should not blossom and there be no fruit on the vines, though the yield of the olive should fail and the fields produce no food, though the flock should be cut off from the fold and there be no cattle in the stalls, yet I will exult in the Lord, I will rejoice in the God of my salvation" (Habakkuk 3:17–18).

But the righteous.

Paris, France

But Peter

Mark 14:66–72

All of us can relate to Simon Peter. He was up and he was down. He spoke when he should have kept quiet, and he kept quiet when he should have spoken. There were days when he was bold as a lion, but there were times when he shied away from young girls.

We could find many words to describe our man Peter: fisherman, disciple, apostle, follower, miracle worker, witness, preacher, and martyr. I'm sure we could list many more.

Perhaps the most noteworthy omission from our list is—are you ready?—backslider! *You've got to be kidding*, some may think. This guy, who declared, "You are the Christ, the Son of the living God" (Matthew 16:16), who preached with great authority on the day of Pentecost (Acts 2), who spoke with great boldness (Acts 4), a backslider? Yes, he's the one.

Perhaps that's why we relate to him so well.

Near the end of Mark's gospel, we read that Jesus was having a meal with his band of followers. Just before they exited the upper room, Jesus told them that He would be betrayed and that all of them would "fall away." When the Shepherd was struck down, the sheep would scatter (14:27).

Peter was the first to declare his loyalty. "Not me, Lord," he said. "All the rest may desert you, but you can count on me. I'll be here to the very end." Yeah, right.

Our Lord replied, "Truly I say to you, that this very night, before a rooster crows twice, you yourself will deny me three times" (14:30).

73

Peter's reaction was quick, pointed, and strong. "Even if I have to die with you, I will not deny you!"

Jump forward for a moment to our text (Mark 14:66–72). After the betrayal of Christ by Judas, Jesus was arrested and carried away. The Shepherd was struck down and the sheep began to scatter, even Peter—or maybe we should say most notably Peter.

Three times Peter was questioned about his identity: "Aren't you a Galilean?" "Didn't I see you with the man Jesus?" "Aren't you one of His followers?" Three times, just as Jesus had said, he denied his relationship with Christ. He even began to curse and to swear (v. 71). Does someone like Peter, or someone like us for that matter, all of a sudden deny the Lord? I don't think so. An old country preacher once remarked, "You don't fall into sin. You slide in!" A current song says, "It's a slow fade."

Before Peter got close to the fire to warm his hands (14:67), his heart was cooling. What were the components that brought on this coldness of heart?

Pride

Bold Peter had thrown down the gauntlet. "All of them may fall away," he said, "but I could never deny you. I am here to the end, Lord." I do not think he visited the ophthalmologist, but Peter had an *I* problem.

Pride has been called a deadly sin, and it will bring you down every time. Wise Solomon wrote, "Pride goes before destruction and a haughty spirit before stumbling" (Proverbs 16:18). Paul would later say, "Therefore let him who thinks he stands take heed lest he fall" (1 Corinthians 10:12). Is there someone reading these words who needs to take heed?

Priorities

When Jesus entered the garden of Gethsemane to agonize in prayer, He took His disciples with Him. His inner circle of Peter, James, and John went with Him a little farther into the garden. Jesus left to pray and three times returned to find His faithful followers sleeping. "C'mon, guys," He pleaded. "Watch and pray. Can't you give up a few minutes?" Something interesting happened. Jesus saw them sleeping, but He said to Peter, "Simon, are you asleep?" Jesus and Peter knew that he was.

Sometimes the road to our own denial of Christ is paved with good intentions but bad application. Peter's priorities were messed up. Are yours?

Performance

The nameless swordsman of verse 47 is Peter. In fact, it was John who told on him (John 18:10)! Instead of being something, Peter resorted to doing something. He forgot that the Lord gave him the be-attitudes, not the do-attitudes!

Many of Christ's followers today do the same thing. They attempt to replace a genuine commitment to the Lord with fleshly conduct. They join a church, sing in a choir, play in a band, or teach a class. All of these things are great; in fact, they are commendable. But you must not merely do something. You must be something. Be that man or woman God has called you to be.

Position

Please forgive me for my spiritual interpretation in this instance. I am sure some critical thinkers, self-appointed theologians, and would-be preachers might chuckle at my handling of this last area. "Improper hermeneutics!" they will scream, and honestly, I concur. Still, I see a larger meaning in the fact that Peter "followed at a distance" (v. 54). He sought to live his Christian life from afar. I've met many like him in my day! They worship, sing, fellowship, give, and serve at a distance. May God help us!

When you add up Peter's pride, priorities, performance, and position, it's no wonder he denied His Lord. It really is true: we, like Peter, don't fall into sin; we slide in.

The one good thing about this story is how it ended. No, I don't mean the denial or the cursing or the roosters. Chapter 14 ends this way: "And he (Peter) began to weep" (v. 72). God would rather that we go through a defeat that leaves us broken than win a victory that leaves us proud.

But Peter.

Timbuktu, Mali

But Malachi

Malachi 1:2, 6-7; 2:17; 3:7-8, 13
(Selected Passages)

The Old Testament book of Malachi is a favorite of many of God's children. It can be read in a matter of minutes. However, it can take a lifetime to understand and to apply all of its teachings. In four short chapters, the prophet delves into topics like God's sovereignty, judgment, discipline, divorce, tithing, and the second coming, just to mention a few.

The name Malachi means "messenger of the Lord." This messenger still has a message worth hearing and heeding. Malachi is the last book of the Old Testament. Some have suggested that it is a "transitional" book, leading us into the New Testament. As you read these words, it's as if the sun had begun to set on a wayward, weary, and corrupt nation.

God had been faithfully speaking through His men and to His people. But the pen was about to be put down, the sound system was being unplugged, and the curtain of God's silence would be pulled shut. God was going to judge His people, not with plagues, floods, or famines, but with silence.

About three hundred years earlier, the farmer/prophet Amos spoke of such a time.

"'Behold, days are coming,' declares the Lord God, 'When I will send a famine on the land, not a famine for bread or a thirst for water, but rather for hearing the words of the Lord'" (Amos 8:11).

Roger D. Mardis

I recall many times in my youth when my disobedience brought on my parents' disgust. I feared the groundings, spankings, timeouts, and loss of some privilege. But one of the toughest parts of their disciplining was their silence. I was forced to think about my sour attitude or my unwise choices. If you've been there, you know silence can resound loudly in the heart, if not in the ears!

Before this four-hundred-year season of silence, God's man delivered to a corrupt people some stern words. God wanted His people then and now to get right, be right, and stay right. He doesn't want us to live in rebellion but in revival. And revival is a theme of this book.

One way we know that we are not walking in a spirit of revival is that we begin to question God. Instead of obeying or responding, we ask, "Why should I have to do that? What good will that do? Where does it say I have to do that?" People living in rebellion and needing revival will question God. Have you ever done that? Well, now you know why.

Malachi recorded God's people asking seven quirky questions, and each time we see our little hinge, *but*, coming into play. Here are the questions:

"'I have loved you,' says the Lord. 'But you say, "How have You loved us?"'" (Malachi 1:2).

"'A son honors his father, and a servant his master. Then if I am a father, where is My honor? And if I am a master, where is My respect?' says the Lord of hosts to you, O priests who despise My name. But you say, 'How have we despised Your name?'" (Malachi 1:6).

"'You are presenting defiled food upon My altar. But you say, 'How have we defiled You?' In that you say, 'The table of the Lord is to be despised'" (Malachi 1:7).

"'You have wearied the Lord with your words. But you say, 'How have we wearied Him?' In that you say, 'Everyone who does evil is good in the sight of the Lord, and He delights in them,' or, 'Where is the God of justice?'" (Malachi 2:17).

"'From the days of your fathers you have turned aside from My statutes and have not kept them. Return to Me, and I will return

80

to you,' says the Lord of hosts. But you say, 'How shall we return?'" (Malachi 3:7).

"Will a man rob God? Yet you are robbing Me! But you say, 'How have we robbed You?' In tithes and offerings" (Malachi 3:8).

"'Your words have been arrogant against Me,' says the Lord. 'But you say, "What have we spoken against You?"'" (Malachi 3:13).

As you read these verses, it's easy to see that God's people doubted His love (1:2), despised His name (1:6), defiled His altar (1:7), disregarded His holiness (2:17), declined His invitation (3:7), depleted His storehouse (3:8), and denied His blessings (3:13).

The inquisitive Bible student would do well to carefully examine all seven of these areas. Each situation is revealing, as is each question. Let me address briefly the last two areas.

Our Giving

One sure way to tell whether people are living in rebellion or walking in revival is their giving practices. Most believers would never consider robbing from one another, but Malachi said they had been robbing God. Not only was this disobedient, but it left them cursed (3:9).

The Lord then revealed the way out of their disobedience. In 3:10 we see the proportion required ("the whole tithe"), the place for it ("into the storehouse"), and the proposition ("test me now in this, says the Lord of hosts"). God says when we do that, He will rebuke our enemy and bless our lives.

Churches that are greatly used by the Lord are full of members who know what it is to give generously and have pastors who preach this truth faithfully.

Our Living

Like God's people in Malachi's day, many in our own wonder if it's worthwhile to serve the Lord. They view life's seeming injustices and inconsistencies and think, *What's the use?* The outcome is that most of America's churches are being served by tired and weary leaders.

Years ago, I heard someone liken the church to a football game. In a football game, you have twenty-two players on the field who need some rest and hundreds or even thousands of people in the bleachers who need some exercise. The average church is similar. It is served by a small group of faithful followers, but most of the others are merely observing from the seats.

Why is that? The reasons may be many, but among them would surely be that people don't think their service is needed, worthwhile, or effective. "It's vain to serve God," is their cry.

As a minister of the gospel for thirty-plus years, I can tell you that your pastor and your church need your support, not your questions. Don't live in rebellion, but experience revival. Not only will you change, but your church will be changed.

But that wasn't the case in Malachi's day.

So what did God do? He stepped back and He stepped away for four hundred years, and His prophets were silent—that is until John came on the scene and said, "Behold the Lamb of God." Jesus is the key to a relationship with God, to righteousness, and to personal revival.

Choose this day not to ask quirky questions. Don't live in rebellion against God. Rather, be a faithful and fruitful child living in the joys of revival.

But Malachi.

Assisi, Italy

But the Prodigal Son

Luke 15:11–24

Luke 15 is one of the great chapters of the Scripture. None of them is bad, but some stand out as favorites of many Christians. Chapters such as Psalm 23, Isaiah 53, John 3, 1 Corinthians 13, Romans 8, Ephesians 1, and Hebrews 11 come to mind. Dr. G. Campbell Morgan once said, "If we were to look for and choose the greatest single chapter in the Bible, you would have to give careful consideration to Luke 15." I certainly concur.

Luke 15 offers a series of illustrations that deal with two categories of lost people. This idea is clearly seen in the opening verse. The tax collectors and sinners (v.1) were lost and they knew it. The Pharisees and scribes (v.2) were lost but thought they were saved. The first group was "coming near to Jesus and listening," but the second group was "grumbling and complaining."

The chapter addresses the crowd of lost humanity, and it does so through one parable with four parts. The chapter moves from lost sheep to lost silver to a lost son and finally to a lost sibling.

It's the third subject, the lost son that we will examine today. Many call this son the Prodigal Son or the wasteful son. He was living in rebellion, waste, and unbelief, "but when he came to his senses" (v. 17) he experienced a defining moment in his life. I have experienced such a moment, and perhaps you have too. Let's follow his story.

His Attitude (vv. 11–12)

This young man was a sinner and he was eaten up with rebellion. This has become common in our day. Young people (and old) rebel against government leaders, church leaders, school leaders, and family leaders.

In effect, the son said, "I want something for nothing. I am due this payment." Jewish law explained a father's disbursements to his sons, but this was to happen "at death" (Deuteronomy 21:17). The son's attitude was unethical and insensitive. He seemed to be telling his dad, "I wish you were dead."

His Actions (vv. 13–14)

Poor attitudes always lead to poor actions. Having gotten his "inheritance," this young boy quickly entered a downward spiral. His pockets were full, but the same couldn't be said of his head or his heart. Having left home, he soon found himself in a distant country. Sometimes you can measure the distance not in miles but in morals!

Sin will take you further than you intended to go (v. 13), it will keep you longer than you intended to stay (v. 13), and it will cost you more than you intended to pay (v. 14). He may have thought everything started so right, but he soon realized things had gone very wrong.

In my years of pastoral ministry, I've met my fair share of prodigals who ended up experiencing the far country. In fact, there was a time in my own life when I found myself in the far country of rebellion. I was constantly in the wrong places with the wrong people and doing the wrong things. Sin promised me freedom, but it gave me only misery. Sin promised success, but it brought only failure. Sin promised enjoyment, but it produced only enslavement!

If you find yourself in that far country, there will come a time when your resources dry up, your so-called friends leave, and you are in want.

His Agony (vv. 14–16)

Rebellion promises much but delivers so little. The prodigal, once the friend of many because of his recent inheritance, had now squandered all of it. He had spent everything, he was now impoverished, and his friends were long gone, leaving him even more quickly than they had come.

In a short time he had gone from the proverbial penthouse to the literal pigpen.

His Acknowledgment (vv. 17–19)

Notice how verse 17 begins: "But … he came to his senses." Perhaps he had what some call a light bulb moment or a wakeup call. Whatever it was, he came to his senses. He changed his mind about himself, his sin, and his situation. "I will get up, I will go, and I will say" (v. 18). That was truly a better place to be.

And notice that he said, "I have sinned" (vv. 18, 21). That is the key. There must come a time in our lives when we agree with God about our sin, forsake it, and move away. I am told that the phrase "I have sinned" is found only eight times in the Bible and that in four of those instances the people didn't mean it! Why so few times? Because it is so hard for us to say, "I have sinned."

His Acceptance (vv. 20–24)

Someone has said this shouldn't be the story of a lousy son but rather of a loving father. When the boy came to his senses, he abandoned his life of waste and came home to the open, loving arms of his dad.

I love verse 20: "While he was still a long way off, his father saw him and felt compassion for him and ran and embraced him and kissed him." As gut-wrenching as it must have been when all his "friends" in the far country left him, it surely was heartwarming when he found the amazing love of his father.

What a father! What a feast! What a forgiveness!

Where do you find yourself today? Are you looking for love in all the wrong places? Have you left the comfort and compassion of home only to end up in a distant land? Are you at a place in life you never dreamed you'd be? If so, the prodigal understands, and so do I.

"But when he came to his senses …" You'll have to do the same. And when you do, you'll find a loving father who has been a "looking father," standing on His tiptoes, scanning the horizon, waiting for you to come home.

The hymn writer said it well: *I've wandered far away from God. Now I'm coming home. The paths of sin too long I've trod. Now I'm coming home. Coming home, coming home, never more to roam. Open wide thine arms of love. Lord, I'm coming home.*

But the Prodigal Son.

Location Unknown

But the Thief

Luke 23:39–43

The *but* of Luke 23:40 may be the most inviting, intriguing, and inspiring of them all. The passage is about our Lord's crucifixion and the similar deaths of two criminals. We often speak of "the thief on the cross." The word Dr. Luke used speaks of one who plunders and steals. He was not a common robber or a petty thief. Rather, he was a cruel bandit who took pleasure in abusing, torturing, and perhaps even killing his victims.

When I was in college, I worked as a part-time disc jockey at a local Southern gospel radio station. One of the often-requested songs we played said, "The one on the right, he was a sinner; the one on the left was too. But the one in the center was a Savior, and He died just to save me and you."

Jesus and the two thieves were going to die on this not-so-good Friday. It has been said that one man died in sin, one died to sin, and one died for sin. While the one sinner was dying in his sin, the other was about to have a change of heart. Notice the word *but* that begins verse 40.

"But the other answered, and rebuking him said, 'Do you not even fear God, since you are under the same sentence of condemnation?'" (Luke 23:40).

This is such an important scene and turn of events that all four gospel writers took time to record aspects of it. This very familiar story has much to say to us. Some people question the validity and

91

authenticity of deathbed conversions. Jesus not only believed this one, but reached out to this dying man.

I can't speak with certainty, but this may have been the thief's first opportunity to hear and trust in Christ. It may have been his only opportunity. One thing I do know is that it was his last opportunity and he made the most of it. I only wish all people today would do the same.

Why this story and why this way? Those are good questions. Let me suggest three reasons.

A Prophetic Reason

Mark's gospel says, "He [Jesus] was numbered with the transgressors" (Mark 15:28). This statement is based on the prophecy of Isaiah in Isaiah 53:12.

A Punishment Reason

Though we don't know the full extent of the thief's crime, evidently it was one worthy of death. Hebrew and Roman law allowed for capital punishment, and these thieves paid dearly.

A Practical Reason

Just think: if this thief had died on any other hill on any other day, he would have died lost in his sin. Some people live in the right place. This man died there! Talk about a captive audience. He heard, saw, and even felt our Lord's passion. You wonder if he hummed the words, "At the cross, at the cross, when I first saw the light and the burden of my heart rolled away ..."

The gospel writers say that for a time this thief, like the other thief and the crowd, was rowdy and cruel and landed some verbal punches on our Lord. Even the passersby hurled abuse. But something began to happen.

What He Saw

The trial, flogging, and crucifixion of Jesus were all obviously unjust. The thief saw all of these events front and center. He also saw the mob casting insults, cursing, and swearing. The crowd cheered and sneered, calling for the death of Jesus.

Perhaps the thief even knew Barabbas, knew he was a criminal but was going free. Jesus now occupied Barabbas's cross. The thief watched all of this unfold before his eyes.

What He Sensed

In three verses of Luke's account our criminal made four statements, which were most revealing.

"Do you not even fear God?" (v. 40). He recognized Christ's deity.

"We are receiving what we deserve" (v. 41). He confessed his own sin and depravity.

"This man has done nothing wrong" (v. 41). He pointed out the Lord's sinlessness.

"Jesus, remember me when You come in Your kingdom" (v. 42). He understood that Christ was a king and was to have a kingdom and would live again after He died. To use our terminology, he asked to be saved.

Paul would later write, "If you confess with your mouth the Lord Jesus, and believe in your heart that God has raised Him from the dead, you will be saved" (Romans 10:9). Here was a man with an amazing boldness and belief, and Jesus responded to him, "Today [not later] you will be with Me in paradise" (v. 43).

Talk about grace; here was a man one or two broken legs from hell and Jesus saved him. In a matter of a few hours, he went from punishment to paradise—once a bandit, but now a believer.

I love the old Negro spiritual that asks, *Were you there when they crucified my Lord? Were you there when they crucified my Lord? Oh, sometimes it causes me to tremble, tremble, tremble. Were you there when they crucified my Lord?*

In one sense all of us were. If this song is ever sung in heaven, do you suppose the thief will bow his head or be moved to tears? May each of us have this thief's boldness and his belief.

But the thief.

Assisi, Italy

But Joshua

Joshua 1:8–9

Transitions can be challenging. You see it when the founder/CEO of a large company retires or dies. The firm must find a successor and the change will be hard. This happens on teams when a long-tenured and successful coach retires to make way for a young upstart who is still wet behind the ears. It happens in churches when a prominent pastor resigns to lead another congregation. When the next shepherd is finally located, it doesn't take long before the comparisons are made.

It also happened to Israel. Moses had led this group out of Egypt and through the wilderness for more than forty years. Sure, the Israelites murmured, complained, and rebelled, but Moses was still their man! When it came time for Moses to die (remember he committed a sin unto death when he struck the rock), God let him see Canaan from the mountaintop, but he couldn't enter. He died on the mountain and God buried him. Yes, Moses was 120 years old, but he was still strong, sharp, and had good eyesight (Deuteronomy 34:4–8).

It was time for a transition to a new leader. Enter Hoshea, better known as Joshua. You think your lot in life is tough? Bet you never followed a guy who got water out of rocks and parted a sea. The transition may have been hard for the people, but it had to be at least as intimidating for Joshua.

God got right to the point: "Moses, My servant is dead" (Joshua 1:2). As the Lord revealed to Joshua His plan and Joshua's part in it, we come to a passage with a now-familiar hinge: "but you shall meditate" on what I'm about to give you, God says.

As Joshua emerged in his new role, God prepared, schooled, and molded this young warrior, telling him three things.

The Truth about Scripture (v. 8)

God had given Moses the books of the Law, and now the Scriptures were being handed down to young Joshua. I'm told that when a president of the United States leaves office one of the last things he does is write a note to his successor. This is an honorable tradition that has been passed on through the years.

What Moses left for Joshua was more than a simple note. It was the inspired Word of God. Joshua was told to memorize it. He was commanded not to let this Word leave his mouth, to keep it, to hide it in his heart. He was also told to meditate on it. The picture here is of an animal called a "ruminant." A ruminant is a mammal that digests its food by initially softening it in the first compartment of its stomach. This compartment is called the rumen. Later the animal regurgitates the partially digested food and "chews the cud." The food is later fully digested through the remaining compartments of the stomach. Cattle, sheep, goats, deer, and antelopes are some of the animals called ruminants.

In the same way, we are told to "bring back up" the memorized Word and to think on it—to chew the cud. The Scripture should also be mastered. The goal is for us to hear, learn, and then apply God's Word. If Joshua was going to succeed in leading God's people, he would have to learn and carry out the Scripture. The same is true for us. Whether we are leading a corporation, a small business, our family, or God's church, we must know the truth about the Scripture.

The Truth about Success (v. 8)

God said Joshua would be successful. We need to be reminded that being successful is not wrong. Some act as if we can't prosper and still be Christians. This is not true.

I want to be successful. I want my family and my children to be successful. I also want you and your family to be successful. *Success* is not a bad word. Granted, we may need to change our definition of success. The world says that to be a success you have to drive a BMW and have a large home, a big bank account, and an ever-expanding 401(k) account. Our world has many people with those things who are miserable. True success for the believer is knowing and doing God's will.

- Joseph understood success.

"The Lord was with Joseph, so he became a successful man. And he was in the house of his master, the Egyptian" (Genesis 39:2).

Success is characterized by God's presence.

- Nehemiah too understood success.

"O Lord, I beseech You, may Your ear be attentive to the prayer of Your servant and the prayer of Your servants who delight to revere Your name, and make Your servant successful today and grant him compassion before this man" (Nehemiah 1:11).

"So I answered them and said to them, 'The God of heaven will give us success; therefore we His servants will arise and build, but you have no portion, right or memorial in Jerusalem'" (Nehemiah 2:20).

Success is a response to prayer.

- Daniel was also successful.

"So this Daniel enjoyed success in the reign of Darius and in the reign of Cyrus the Persian" (Daniel 6:28).

Success is the result of God's protection.

- Joshua would also be successful.

"This book of the law shall not depart from your mouth, but you shall meditate on it day and night, so that you may be careful to do according to all that is written in it; for then you will make your way prosperous, and then you will have success" (Joshua 1:8).

Success is founded on God's promises.

Oh how I pray we will all understand success from God's standpoint and will pursue it with every fiber of our being!

The Truth about Security

Joshua was at a new place in his life, and so were the people he led. There would certainly be some highs and lows, some rainy days and Mondays to get him down. To prepare Joshua for those days and those difficulties, God made a bold declaration: you can go to any place (vv. 2–4), you can stand before any person (v. 5), and you can overcome any problem (vv. 6–7, 9). Three times God said, "Be strong" and "Be courageous." Though Moses was gone, God would be with Joshua wherever he went (v. 9).

Maybe you find yourself in transition. It might be in your job, your marriage, your school, or your ministry. Life's uncertainty and man's inability can be quite disturbing. When you find yourself on the banks of your tomorrow, remember the awesome promises God gave to Joshua—and through Joshua to you.

But Joshua.

Paris, France

But Judas

John 12:4

I've pastored or served the local church for more than three decades. Whatever the city, the state, or the size of the ministry, I've found that folks are folks wherever you go. They might be city folks or country folks, rich folks or poor folks, educated folks or uneducated folks, but they were all still folks.

And every place I've been seems to have some of the same folks in attendance. I once asked a man, "Did you follow me here? I thought you were a member of my last church." Some of you are laughing because you've met them too!

You'll find three types of people in almost every church. Some are crusty, some are cranky, and some are critical. And boy, do they know how to be critical! You've seen them, heard them, prayed for them. You may even have been one of them. Surely not you or me!

I attend the Baptist church, so I won't talk about the others. As for us Baptists, while we may not cuss, we sure do fuss! And we can fuss with the best of them.

We fuss about the schedule, the carpet, the bulletin, and the dress code. Baptist folks get worked up over the temperature in the auditorium, the hats worn by kids, and the teenagers using their cell phones in church. (But they have downloaded their Bibles onto their cell phones, they tell us. Yeah, right!)

But the one area that riles us the most is worship—you know, the hand-raising, hand-clapping, drum-beating, guitar-playing, chorus-singing worship service. A lot of Baptists are critical of worship. Amazing!

So was Judas. Yeah, that Judas! John 12 tells an interesting story. Jesus was visiting a certain home and many people were there. Among them were the disciples and Lazarus, Martha, and Mary. Now remember what had just happened. Lazarus, who had been dead, was now alive. His sisters, Martha and Mary, were thrilled. A meal was prepared and the celebration was on. Before long, the supper turned into a worship service led by Mary.

Mary brought to her Lord a God-honoring offering of fragrant oil and poured it on His feet. As the aroma filled the room, she wiped Jesus' feet with her hair. Her spontaneous act of worship was not on the schedule or in the bulletin. Surely all who saw it were moved.

But not Judas.

He wasn't upset or critical because of what Mary said or sang. He had a problem with what she shared. She was so overwhelmed by all her Lord had done for her and her family that she brought an offering and lavished it upon Him. Judas, the treasurer of the disciples, saw this as poor stewardship. "What a waste," he said. "We've got people starving to death, and she pours out this costly perfume. Unbelievable."

Unbelievable? That's a good description of such fault-finding. And it happens across our land every week as so-called Christians criticize acts of worship. Let me tell you something about these critics.

Critics Can Look Spiritual (v. 4)

Judas was a disciple, a follower, and he looked the part—so much so that when it came time for the twelve to elect officers, Judas, the future traitor, was made treasurer. It's been my experience that those writing the checks, handling the money, and paying the bills for the church are super trustworthy. The disciples thought this of Judas. In fact, when Jesus told the twelve that He would be betrayed, no one suspected Judas. At least he looked spiritual.

Critics Can Sound Spiritual (v. 5)

I've heard them and you have too. You'd think they drink communion juice at every meal they're so holy! "We've got to be good stewards, you know," they will say. "Have we even prayed this through? Did God tell us to do that?" Sounds spiritual, huh?

I recall a time when a gentleman stood up during a rather nasty business conference at church. He had worn his best suit, carefully planned his remarks, and delivered stinging criticism. He had drunk the Judas juice. Have you?

Critics Can Act Spiritual (v. 6)

The Scripture says Judas held the box. He occupied a strategic position. He acted spiritual, and people bought in to his deception.

The same thing happens in our churches. Many have people who sing and serve, who give and go. They watch the nursery and work with teenagers. They even teach and preach, but sometimes all they are doing is acting spiritual.

Critics Will Be Exposed as Unspiritual (v. 4)

Judas intended to betray Jesus, and that is exactly what he did. Mark describes what happened when Judas made his decision.

"Then Judas Iscariot, who was one of the twelve, went off to the chief priests in order to betray Him to them. They were glad when they heard this, and promised to give him money. And he began seeking how to betray Him at an opportune time" (Mark 14:10–11).

Today, we say, "Give them enough rope and they'll hang themselves." If Judas was given enough power or money or influence, he would sell his own soul.

Now, I'm not issuing a blanket condemnation. Not every church member who has criticized a song or a sermon is a Judas. I am simply admonishing you to be careful with your critical words. You are on dangerous ground when you question someone's motives and criticize the way a person worships.

But Judas.

Assisi, Italy

But the Godly Man

Psalm 1:1–3

No doubt you know that the book of Psalms was the original Hebrew hymnbook. One fact you may not know is that the first two psalms are "orphans." They are called that because no human author is named. Perhaps they were penned by David, Solomon, Asaph, or the sons of Korah. We don't know for certain.

Psalm 1 is about the Law. Psalm 2 has to do with prophecy. Isn't that interesting? This grand book of glorious worship is founded on the Law and the prophets!

Psalm 1 has become one of those dearly loved passages that even most marginal church folks are familiar with. Though it is only six verses, this psalm is substantive, contrasting the godly man and the wicked man. One has a firm and faith-filled life; the other's life is faulty and futile. One is prosperous, while the other is poisonous. One is full of life, and the other is about death.

Examining the worldly and wicked man serves little purpose. We would do better to view the choices and the outcomes of a life lived God's way.

What traits can we see in people who order their lives according to God's plan? The unnamed hymn writer points to four areas in the godly life.

A Principled Life (vv. 1–2)

All of us have guidelines, principles we live by—some good and some bad. We know that there are certain things godly people do and don't do, watch and don't watch, say and don't say. These choices protect them.

The psalmist says we should guard ourselves against negative influences (v. 1), telling us not to "walk in the counsel of the wicked," "stand in the path of sinners," or "sit in the seats of the scoffer." If we listen to bad counsel, we will make bad choices and have bad outcomes every time.

Rather, we should pursue positive influences (v. 2). Instead of denying the Lord, we should delight in Him and in His Word.

"Delight yourself in the Lord; and He will give you the desires of your heart" (Psalm 37:4).

"But his delight is in the law of the Lord, and in His law he meditates day and night" (Psalm 1:2).

Godly men and women love the Lord and His Word, and they can't get enough of either. I'm amazed at people who say they are Bible-believing Christians but don't like spending time with the Lord and in His law. Is yours a principled life?

A Planted Life (v. 3)

We live in a transient world and are constantly on the go. Modern man knows little of stability and longevity. But the psalmist says that the blessed and happy life is a planted or settled life. The godly man will send down deep roots.

Getting planted is important. Your strength, stability, and very survival are at stake. Where you get planted is crucial. Soil and moisture and mineral content are all important to the growth and health of your "tree." Don't settle for the devil's desert or the world's wasteland. Plant yourself by the rivers of living water!

As a pastor, I see a popular but alarming trend. So-called spiritual people no longer see the need for corporate worship or for church membership. The New Testament sees a Christian's life as inseparable from a local church. For years I've told people they need three homes: an earthly home, a heavenly home, and a church home. Find one and get planted!

A Productive Life (v. 3)

The godly life produces fruit, and its leaf does not wither. I like that, don't you? In fact, I don't just like it; I want that fruitful and faithful life. In the New Testament, we learn of the "fruit of the Spirit." Here is what Paul said:

"But the fruit of the Spirit is love, joy, peace, patience, kindness, goodness, faithfulness, gentleness, self-control; against such things there is no law" (Galatians 5:22–23).

Jesus also talked about the "fruit that remains." Read His words.

"You did not choose Me but I chose you, and appointed you that you would go and bear fruit, and that your fruit would remain, so that whatever you ask of the Father in My name He may give to you" (John 15:16).

Is that your life? The godly man will be fruitful and faithful.

A Prosperous Life (v. 3)

Someone once said, "It pays to follow Jesus." And it does. Now don't misunderstand me. I'm not saying that if you love Jesus, learn His Word, and are planted by the streams of living water you'll have a big house, a fancy car, and a sizable bank account. That's not what the psalmist said, and it's not what I'm saying.

But I believe in the blessing and favor of God. When you live your life according to God's plan, you will be in a position to know His blessing on your marriage, your family, your work, your children, and your grandchildren. You name it and God can bless it.

But the godly man.

Florence, Italy

But Michal

2 Samuel 6

Few passages in the Bible have challenged and intrigued me more through the years than our text for today. It's a story of praise, worship, and a vocal critic. Christianity and churches have never been without their critics, especially when it comes to the practices of praise and worship.

The background of our story can be seen in 1 Chronicles 13–15. Perhaps you'll want to take a few minutes to familiarize yourself with these happenings.

The Scripture reminds us that the Ark of the Covenant had been stolen. Can you imagine the symbol of God's presence, the place where the blood was poured out, the holder of the stone tablets, the golden pot of manna, and Aaron's budding rod taken by the enemies of God, leaving Israel with a mere reminder of what used to be? The ark is also an Old Testament picture of the coming Lord Jesus.

King David was confronted with this tragedy, and then he did something about it. You might say that in the beginning he did the right thing but went about it in the wrong way. Sound familiar? Sometimes we in the modern church do the same.

David finally got it right, teaching us several things crucial to meaningful worship. First, it is founded on the Scripture (1 Chronicles 15:13–15). David now desired to act according to the Word of God, not the ways of man. We would do well to learn from that! Second, it is full of singing (1 Chronicles 15:16–28). Don't you love being in a place where people are uninhibited about singing to the Lord? When God fills your heart, His praise will flow from your mouth. Third, it is focused on sacrifice. The blood was poured out. You can't have worship without it. Fourth, it is free and spontaneous. Perhaps this was David's "Hebrew shake." Whatever you call it, David and the others celebrated in and because of the Lord's presence. Great time, huh?

But Michal (2 Samuel 6:20)

As David returned to Jerusalem with the ark, his bride watched him from a window. Was she mad? Embarrassed? Jealous? What was the deal with Michal? The Bible says, "When she saw David leaping and celebrating, she despised him in her heart" (1 Chronicles 15:29). What? You have got to be kidding.

I've met a few Michals in my day, and I'm sure you have too. When God begins to move in a significant way, His presence infuses a church with freshness and power, the worship and praise become animated and spontaneous. Those things bring out man's best, and sadly, his worst.

David Rebuked Her (2 Samuel 6:21)

The king was quick to point out, "I didn't do this for you, sister. I did it for the Lord. He chose me and called me. I will celebrate before the Lord." We would all do well to learn from David's words and actions.

God Judged Her (2 Samuel 6:23)

David's response was bad enough, but now Michael faced the wrath of almighty God. As the Lord had brought Uzziah low, His holy judgment now hit Michal. He took away her ability to bear children. In that culture and setting, death would have been easier.

The Nation Forgot Her

After this, Michal dropped from the pages of Holy Scripture. This woman, once the nation's first lady, became the forgotten lady. You better be careful when you criticize a fresh move by God. There are numerous Michals today who despise what the Lord is doing in our midst.

There are several noteworthy points about this lady Michal. She was Saul's daughter, the child of a king (1 Samuel 14:49). She was David's wife, the bride of a king (1 Samuel 18:27). She was purchased with blood. David gained her from Saul when he presented the foreskins of two hundred dead Philistines (1 Samuel 18:20–29). Though she was the child of a king and the bride of a king, bought with blood, she despised what the king was doing in her presence.

We too are children of the King, the bride of Christ, and we've been redeemed with the precious blood of Christ. When the Lord begins to do fresh work in our midst, when the praise becomes powerful and the worship becomes wonderful, we better be careful about what we think, say, or do. Our King is watching and listening.

But Michal.

Agra, India

But the Impossible

Mark 10:27

We have read about the man we call the rich young ruler (Mark 10:17–22). You'll recall how he asked the Lord about eternal life and how he could gain it. Jesus told him to "go sell all you own, give the proceeds to the poor, and follow me." At this point our big door slammed shut. "But at these words he was saddened and he went away grieved for he was one who owned much property."

The Great Physician knows exactly the problem with our sinful hearts, so He is sure to prescribe the appropriate meds. Not every patient is in love with his stuff or has a worldly heart, but when your god is your possessions or your wealth, the Great Physician will tell you to "go sell all you have" so you can get a new God.

In the context of that inquiry, Christ gave an illustration, painting for His disciples a picture they no doubt would understand. He said, "It is easier for a camel to go through the eye of a needle than for a rich man to enter the Kingdom of God" (Mark 10:25). Granted, many far-fetched ideas have developed from this verse. Some teach that there was an "after hours" gate in the wall around Jerusalem called the "eye of the needle." When merchants or residents entered town after hours, they would use this gate. To gain access, a man would get off of his camel, remove all of his belongings from the camel's back, place the camel on its knees, and pull it through the opening. Sounds interesting, but there is not and never was a gate by that name. Other tales about this phrase are equally untrue.

Here is a good rule of thumb I learned in seminary: when the plain sense makes good sense, look for no other sense. The plain sense is that it is impossible for a camel to go through the eye of a needle, and it is impossible for a person to get to heaven based on wealth or by any means other than Jesus Christ. You can't buy your way there, work your way there, or be good enough to deserve to be there. Jesus is not the best way to heaven; He is the only way!

In that light we come to today's *but*. Read the close of this encounter: "Looking at them, Jesus said, with people it is impossible but not with God, for all things are possible with God" (Mark 10:27).

All things are possible with God. As long as we look to man's ways, plans, programs, or theories, the desired spiritual outcome is not just improbable but impossible. We can't do God's thing man's way and get God's result. Never. It is impossible.

But when we do God's thing God's way, we get God's perfect outcome. Every time. Here are a few examples;

- Remember when Jesus fed the five thousand-plus with five loaves and two fishes? All things are possible with God.
- Remember when Jesus delivered the man of Gadara who was tormented with a legion of demons? All things are possible with God.
- Do you recall how the Lord rescued the disciples, who were being tossed about in the boat on the sea during a storm and feared they would die? All things are possible with God.
- What about the woman who had a bloody problem for years and had spent all her resources on doctors' care but only grew worse? Remember how she was cured? All things are possible with God.
- How about Mary and Martha, distraught that Jesus wasn't around when their brother Lazarus had fallen ill and died? Do you recall that story? All things are possible with God.

What hurt, habit, or hang-up are you facing? What is the problem, predicament, or peril confronting you? How about the demand, deadline, or disease? Remember this: with men a solution is impossible (your camel of a problem never will go through life's needle!), but the impossible becomes possible when you trust in God. All things are possible with God.

Let me share a personal story. When the Lord moved my family to our current city of residence, I made a quick, impatient, and unwise decision. Instead of waiting on the Lord's timing and perfect will, I put a contract on a house that I should never have bought. It was a beautiful home in an awesome neighborhood with fantastic neighbors. My problem was with an unethical agent who sold me the money pit. I'll spare you the details.

Long story short, I hated this home and wanted out. The expense, frustration, and upkeep were taking their toll on my time, my health, and my marriage, but we were stuck.

During this time, my wife and I attended a pastors' getaway in Colorado with some dear friends from *Shepherd's Haven of Rest Ministries*. On our last night there we had a prayer meeting with our hosts, and we discussed and prayed over our house issue. My wife said, "I just wish God would send someone our way to say they want to buy our house." Like Sarah when she heard the news of a coming baby, I chuckled.

Our house was not on the market, and the local unemployment rate was soaring as the nation experienced the economic troubles of 2008–09. This was not a promising picture. But …

One Saturday morning I was home alone. Michelle was at the store and our children were at a Disciple Now event. At about 10 a.m. my phone rang. It was a friend who is a real estate agent. "Roger," she said, "are you interested in selling your home? I have a client who is looking for your size home in our city, and we've exhausted all our options in the market." Within thirty-six hours we had in hand a signed contract. Sarah shouldn't have laughed, and neither should I. Why? All things are possible with God.

What is it in your life, business, marriage, or church that looks less than promising? It might be a health issue, a financial issue, or a family issue. Remember, with people a solution is impossible but not with God, for all things are possible with God.

I love the closing scene of the movie *Facing the Giants*. After his team wins an improbable state football championship, Coach Grant Taylor goes around the locker room asking his jubilant players, "Is there anything God can't do?" And of course the answer is, "Nothing, Coach."

But the impossible.

Assisi, Italy

But Be Transformed

Romans 12:2

My wife and I have four children. The first three were boys and then we had our girl. (Did I mention anything about drama?) During our children's formative years, we learned about Transformers. One of the boys must have introduced us to them, but I'm not sure. I don't even recall what Transformers were. I just remember we had to have them.

You and I may not be Transformers, but God wants us to undergo a transformation. Today's passage should be familiar. Perhaps it is one you have committed to memory or have studied. If so, you've no doubt learned about metamorphosis or the act of transforming. Let's examine this verse.

"And do not be conformed to this world, but be transformed by the renewing of your mind, so that you may prove what the will of God is, that which is good and acceptable and perfect" (Romans 12:2).

Don't Be Conformed

Paul is saying, "Don't let the world squeeze you into its mold." Yet we see that happening more and more in our churches and our families. We don't mean to let this happen, but when we look back over our lives, we see that the world has us in its grip. So many lives look more like the world than they do the Word.

It's a slow and subtle process. We become friends with the world (James 4:4), then we love the world (1 John 2:15), and finally we're conformed to the world (Romans 12:2). It is so easy to veer off the narrow path; we then become vulnerable to the attractions of the world and wind up victims.

Have you ever seen this happen? I've witnessed this "moving away" in many lives. It all begins with a single step in the wrong direction. A classic example is Lot in the Old Testament. He was Abraham's nephew. Lot started right, but went wrong in a hurry.

Lot "pitched his tent toward Sodom" (Genesis 13:12). Then we find Lot "living in Sodom" (Genesis 14:12). Before you know it, he was "sitting in the gate" (Genesis 19:1). First he was hesitant, then resident, and finally president! The world had put a vise on Lot's soul and squeezed him into submission.

But Be Transformed

The word Paul uses is *metamorphosis*. It is the process that changes an egg to a caterpillar and a caterpillar to a butterfly. This is a radical and dramatic change. And God demands the same of His followers.

This transformation is fascinating to watch or to study. It takes time. A butterfly's egg will hatch out in three to seven days. Young caterpillars eat nonstop for the next few weeks and grow substantially. Then they attach themselves to a branch or a stem and spin their own silk to form a chrysalis. From this tomb-like encasement, a beautiful butterfly will emerge in about two weeks. The entire process is called metamorphosis.

The change requires toughness. When the young butterfly emerges from its cocoon, it releases hormones that aid in the hardening of its tender wings and enable it to fly. God has so designed the development of the butterfly that it needs this struggle from the cocoon to release the hormones. The butterfly may not like the struggle, but it is necessary.

We too may not like the struggles we face or the storms we endure, but we need them. God uses such events to develop and mature His children. Do you want to crawl around like a worm or fly like a butterfly? Learning to fly takes time and toughness.

And Be Reformed

Once transformed, the growing disciple will begin to know and to follow God's will. Paul says of the Lord's will for us, "It is good and acceptable and perfect." The word *reformed* means to have been changed from a worse to a better state. A reformation is a beneficial change.

In Romans 12:1, Paul discusses living sacrifices—the kind that have a tendency to crawl off of the altar! Ever done that? I have. Paul also says of our bodies that they must be "holy and acceptable." That should go without saying: if something is not holy, it's not acceptable.

Don't let the fatal attractions of this world catch your eye or your heart. If you allow that to happen, the world will squeeze you into its mold.

But be transformed.

Munich, Germany

But Not All Things Are Profitable

1 Corinthians 6:12

I've pastored long enough to have been asked most questions. "Why can't I do this?" "Why can't we go there?" I'm still learning, but not all vices or evils are specifically addressed in Scripture, not by a strict "thou shalt" or "thou shalt not." But they are addressed by way of principles.

The Bible by and large is not a book of rules, but of principles. If it were a book of rules, it would be so large that none of us could carry it around. If it were a book of rules, it would not be relevant to all cultures or generations. Some laws of yesteryear are no longer needed or practical. Also, one might find a loophole in a rule. But this is never true of a principle.

Laws are many. Principles are few. Laws often change; principles never do. I like that!

Yes, there are rules in the Bible, and we should do our best to honor our Lord and to obey His Word. There are things we shall and shall not do.

What about those places some call gray areas? If there is no clear command or prohibition, how does one make a proper decision? That may be an easier question to ask than to answer.

Here is Paul's admonition to the struggling and immature Corinthian church: "All things are lawful for me, but not all things are profitable" (1 Corinthians 6:12).

The word *profitable* should lead us to ask an important question. That is, where will an action take me? The apostle is saying, "Though something may not necessarily be morally wrong for me to do, neither will it help get me to my desired destination or outcome." That's crucial!

Why is this so important? There seem to be a lot of gray doors swinging today, and going through them won't help us get to our goal of Christ-likeness. Early in our Christian life and walk we need to incorporate the principles we will live by and to decide on the questions we need to ask as we attempt to make wise decisions.

Will This Get Me Somewhere? (1 Corinthians 6:12)

If I choose to do or not do a particular thing, will this help or hinder my spiritual growth? Will this thing help me reach my spiritual goals? The writer of Hebrews spoke of encumbrances and sins that entangle (12:1–2). One will slow you down, but the other will trip you up.

Will It Lead to Blessing or to Bondage? (1 Corinthians 6:12)

If I make this choice, will it trap me or lead to my enslavement? You are to have but one master, the Lord. Don't let your desires, your lust, your cravings, or your appetites for evil lead to your bondage.

Will It Hurt My Witness? (1 Corinthians 8:8–13)

If I choose a particular thing or course, will it hurt others? Will it harm my testimony for Christ if someone sees me involved in a certain activity? When it comes to life's choices, what kind of example am I setting for my children, my neighbors, my co-workers, and my peers, not to mention lost humanity?

Will the Choice Build Me Up? (1 Corinthians 10:23)

Paul says that not all things "edify." An edifice is a fine building. Some choices *construct us*; they build us up, develop us for good, and make us look worthwhile. Other choices *condemn us*. When we make such choices, we allow the wrecking ball of life to break down or destroy our spiritual influence. Every decision we make builds up or tears down.

Will This Choice Honor Christ? (1 Corinthians 10:31)

Paul says that all we do honors or dishonors our Lord. With every choice I make, God is either glorified or grieved. That's pretty simple, wouldn't you say? If everyone first asked, "Will doing this bring God glory?," I suspect that many lives and choices would change.

Will This Keep Others from Salvation? (1 Corinthians 10:32–33)

We should never involve ourselves in any activity that would cause someone else not to trust our Lord. What we do should point others to Christ. Not only are we to be His witnesses, but we should be part of the evidence!

Would I Want to Be Doing This When the Lord Returns? (1 Corinthians 15:51-52)

I believe our Lord is coming again—soon. In fact, I've quit looking for signs… I'm listening for sounds! Would you want to be raptured while watching an immoral movie or hanging out in an evil location? Would you want the Master to return and find you up to your waist in wickedness? Of course you wouldn't. But many so-called believers live their lives in utter rebellion and push the envelope with their actions. One day the Bridegroom will come.

Roger D. Mardis

Here is my challenge. All things are lawful, but not all things are profitable, so ask yourself some simple questions When you need to make choices; especially in those gray areas of life:

- Will this get me somewhere?
- Will it lead to blessing or to bondage?
- Will it hurt my witness?
- Will it build me up or tear me down?
- Will it honor my Lord?
- Will it hinder others from being saved?
- Would I want to be involved in such activity when Jesus returns?

If we aren't careful, we can destroy in a matter of moments what it took us years to build.

But not all things are profitable.

Rome, Italy

But the Resurrection

Luke 24:1; 1 Corinthians 15:13-20

The resurrection of Jesus Christ from the dead has been debated, discussed, and denied by many for years, but it has never been disproved. All one would have to do to wipe out Christianity and destroy the integrity of God's Word, the Bible, is to produce the body of Jesus. It is a fact of history that the man Jesus lived, so if He never rose from the dead, where is His body? Where are His remains? Show me either and I'll stop writing today.

Many have sought to disprove the claims for Christ. There is the swoon theory: Jesus didn't really die, but merely passed out, and once in the tomb, He came to. There is the wrong-tomb theory: the women, and later the disciples, went to the wrong tomb, and that's why it was empty. There is the hallucination theory: Jesus didn't rise from the dead, but the women and the disciples, under great stress to believe His claims, thought they saw Him alive. These are three of the most common theories of unbelieving men. They are theories, not truth. Again I say, produce the body of Jesus.

In Luke's gospel, we find Christ being betrayed, arrested, falsely accused, mocked, beaten, crucified, buried, and raised! Read these words:

"But on the first day of the week, at early dawn, they came to the tomb bringing the spices which they had prepared. And they found the stone rolled away from the tomb, but when they entered, they did not find the body of the Lord Jesus" (Luke 24:1–3).

Christ's bodily resurrection from the dead is a fact of the Bible, and it is fundamental to our belief and to our understanding of the gospel. This element of Christian teaching is not just important; it is imperative. The resurrection is either the greatest event in the history of man or it is the biggest hoax we have ever believed.

Paul the apostle stresses the importance of the resurrected Lord He met on the road to Damascus. In 1 Corinthians 15, Paul develops this theme passionately; in doing so he presents two profound arguments.

But if There Is No Resurrection
(1 Corinthians 15:12–19)

Many Corinthian believers were struggling to grasp this teaching about Christ and their own resurrection. Paul told them, "If there is no resurrection," then several consequences follow.

The Savior (v. 13): If there is no resurrection and no afterlife experience, then not even Christ has been raised. The Jesus some of them saw, knew, heard, and watched was now dead, and He was not coming back.

The Scripture (v. 14): If there is no resurrection, then the preaching ministry is worthless. The Bible would be a lie and Jesus would be a liar. Services, songs, and sermons would all be a waste of time if Jesus were still dead.

Our salvation (v. 14): Without Christ's resurrection and the hope for our own, we could not be saved. Christ was raised for our justification, and our faith in this reality results in our salvation (Romans 10:9–10). If there is no resurrection, we couldn't be saved and might not even want to be. What would be the use?

Our sins (v. 17): If Jesus' body is still in the grave, then you and I are still in our sins. We would be hopelessly lost and unable to right our wrongs. If we are still in our sins, we still have to pay for them.

Man's state (v. 18): Many in the Corinthian church had passed away, and those in this church had also lost Christian family members elsewhere. If there was no resurrection, then any hope of seeing their deceased loved ones alive again was futile. Their bodies would merely decompose and smell.

Our sorrow (v. 19): Paul says that if we have believed a lie, reported an event that never happened, and bought into a great hoax; we should be pitied because we've been duped. All that and so much more follows if there is no resurrection.

But Christ Has Been Raised (1 Corinthians 15:20).

There are many good reasons to believe that Christ was raised from the dead. The Bible declares it so, history has not proven otherwise, we have the eyewitness testimony of many in the first century, and the tradition of the evangelical church has reported this event to be so. Christ Himself said He would be raised.

One day in Athens, Paul was preaching about the resurrection. He said God gave proof of man's salvation by raising Jesus from the dead (Acts 17:31). Yet notice the reaction of his listeners and what followed.

"Now when they heard of the resurrection of the dead, some began to sneer, but others said, 'We shall hear you again concerning this.' So Paul went out of their midst. But some men joined him and believed, among whom also were Dionysius the Areopagite and a woman named Damaris and others with them" (Acts 17:32–34).

There you have it, potential reactions to the resurrection. Some despised; they began to criticize and to sneer. Some delayed, saying, "I'm not sure I want to believe this now, but I may consider these claims one day." Some decided; they believed Paul's message and got involved in his movement.

I'm reminded of the words of the classic hymn:

> *He lives, He lives,*
> *Christ Jesus lives today.*
> *He walks with me, and talks with me,*
> *Along life's narrow way.*
> *He lives, He lives,*
> *Salvation to impart.*
> *You ask me how I know He lives.*
> *He lives within my heart.*

But the resurrection.

Assisi, Italy

But Diotrephes

3 John 9

The third epistle of John is short, but it is significant and substantial. Some theologians have noted that 3 John is the shortest book in the New Testament. Not so, you say; 2 John has thirteen verses and 3 John has fourteen or fifteen depending on your translation. But in the Greek text in which it was originally written, 3 John is the shortest. Gotcha! Both of these epistles have fewer than three hundred words and could have been penned on a single piece of papyrus. That says something to me about the Holy Spirit's overriding purpose and His protection of God's Word!

The third epistle of John is the most personal of the apostle's three letters. The first was more general and was sent to Christian assemblies around Asia Minor. The second was penned to a "lady and her children" (perhaps signifying a house church and its members). John 3 was written to a single recipient by the name of Gaius.

Gaius was as common a name in that era as Bill or Bob would be today. Gaius was John's "son or child" (v. 4) in the Lord's work, and the apostle greatly loved him. In fact, he calls him "beloved" four times (vv. 1, 2, 5, 11).

The purpose of John's letter was not only to encourage Gaius but to expose a crooked man in the church named Diotrephes. John's letter has a sweet and positive tone until verse 9: "but Diotrephes."

Who was this man? What was he doing? What was John's reaction to him, and what would John do? These are good questions and must be answered by the church now. That's because there are plenty like Diotrephes today!

People like this man attend most of our churches. Their nature is the same as his. In fact, most of the churches I've served have had their share of these folks. Let's see, there was Joe, there was Billy, and there was Ed. (The names have been changed so as not to humiliate the guilty and to protect the author!) They are men and sometimes women who are critical, controlling, and caustic; surely you've met them. So had John, and the man's name was Diotrephes.

Historians tell us that this name appears throughout secular Greek literature. It is a name identified with the Greek aristocracy, the noble class. This man was upper class and elite. He was accustomed to the spotlight; he liked special attention and favors. He wanted to do more than run the church. He wanted to ruin it (That's what happens when *I* gets involved!)

Have you ever met someone like this man? Is there a Diotrephes in your life, church, or ministry? Do his ways resemble yours in any respect? Let's see what his résumé shows.

He Had to Be in Charge (v. 9)

John said of him, "He loves to be first among them." That is, Diotrephes had to be in control. He wasn't content merely to be on the board. He had to be the chairman. It was his way and no other.

The church has only one head, and that is not a pastor, a chairman, or a member. Christ is the head of the body of the church. Read Paul's words in Colossians 1:15–18.

"He is the image of the invisible God, the firstborn of all creation. For by Him all things were created, both in the heavens and on earth, visible and invisible, whether thrones or dominions or rulers or authorities—all things have been created through Him and for Him. He is before all things, and in Him all things hold together. He is also head of the body, the church; and He is the beginning, the firstborn from the dead, so that He Himself will come to have first place in everything."

Jesus is the first, the head, the leader; He is the preeminent one!

He Was Not Teachable (v. 9)

John said Diotrephes "does not accept what we say." He was not open to teaching, training, encouragement, or rebuke. He turned a deaf ear to John's words. There are scores of people like that in our churches today. They usually say something like, "Well, I'm just not getting fed." I challenge you to try to "feed" someone with a closed mind, heart, and spirit!

He Accused with Wicked Words (v. 10)

Diotrephes was also making critical statements and false accusations and using wicked words. The term John uses, *prating*, is interesting. The root word means to bubble up, like an air, water, or soap bubble. A bubble has been called a little something surrounding nothing. Empty words. False accusations. I remind you that Satan is called "the accuser of the brethren" (Revelation 12:10).

He Did Not Receive the Brethren (v. 10)

John commended Gaius for his spirit of hospitality toward the traveling teachers and preachers of the gospel. But not Diotrephes. He was a man who had no heart for or interest in missions or ministry. He didn't even care for the men and women of God who came through his village and visited his church. Diotrephes was one miserable old grouch (or maybe he was a young grouch!), and he wanted to be sure everyone else was just as miserable. You better watch out for his kind.

He Was Hostile to the Hospitable (v. 10)

Diotrephes was opposed not only to visitors but to those who helped and hosted them. John said, "He puts them out of the church."

In that sense Diotrephes was a CEO—the chief expulsion officer. Miserable people seldom want ministering people around. Just saying!

I like John's words: "I will call attention to his deeds." The Diotrepheses of this world will not quit or quiet down. They have to be recognized, rebuked, and removed from our midst.

Before closing his brief letter to Gaius, John commended a man named Demetrius (v. 12). He was a member whom everyone knew, loved, respected, and appreciated. So John told Gaius, "Don't imitate Diotrephes. Be like Demetrius. Don't hinder God's work. Help it. Don't be a liability to your church. Be an asset."

That is still good advice for us today.

But Diotrephes.

Beijing, China

But Temptations

1 Corinthians 10:13

Chapter 10 of Paul's first epistle to the Corinthians is interesting and valuable. He reminds us to avoid doing the same sinful things the nation of Israel did. In fact, he says, Israel's failures should be an example to us and teach us some of life's lessons (v. 11).

This chapter has much to say about idolatry and immorality. As one pastor said, "These two are notorious companions." Since the Enemy can't have your spirit, he will go after the other two-thirds of you—your soul (mind, will, and emotions) and your body. So before your soul he dangles the carrot of idolatry and before your body the carrot of immorality.

Temptations in and of themselves are not sins. Jesus was led by the Spirit into the wilderness to be tempted by the devil (Matthew 4:1). The writer of Hebrews says, "For we do not have a High Priest who cannot sympathize with our weaknesses, but one who has been tempted in all things as we are, yet without sin." (4:15). The problems come when we yield to temptations. Jesus never yielded.

As Paul recounts the ups and downs of Israel, he reminds us that we don't have to make the same mistakes the Hebrews made. Temptation may come knocking, but we don't have to answer the door! The key to our understanding of this subject and to our victory is found in our focal passage.

"No temptation has ever taken you but such as is common to man; and God is faithful, who will not allow you to be tempted beyond what you are able, but with the temptation will provide (for you) a way of escape, so that you will be able to endure it" (1 Corinthians 10:13).

This verse tells me at least four things concerning temptations.

Temptations Are Universal, Not Unique

Paul said all men (and women) face temptation. I have been to four of the seven continents. My seminary said to travel "to all the world for Jesus' sake," so I am trying to do my part! I hope to travel to all seven—well, maybe six. I'll leave Antarctica to the Eskimo missionaries.

In my travels I've learned that folks are folks wherever you go. Whatever their color or culture or caste, men and women struggle with issues of idolatry and immorality everywhere. I've seen it in the squatter villages of South Africa and in the homes of wealthy businessmen. I've found it to be true in the rural villages of Moldova and in the booming metropolis of Beijing. It's true in Alaska, Canada, and Guatemala. I've seen firsthand the results of poor choices in the lives of Cubans and Jamaicans.

Sin's lure truly is common to humanity.

Temptations Are Conquerable, Not Consuming

The text says that God "will not allow you to be tempted beyond what you are able." Sometimes we get confused about trials and temptations. God tests us to bring out our best. Satan tempts us to bring out our worst. The Lord wants to develop us, but the Enemy wants to destroy us.

God put limits on what Satan could do to Job, on how far he could go with him, and the Lord has established similar limits for us. On a large ship there is a mark called the Plimsoll line. This line is there to show the captain and the crew when they've reached their load limit. When the Plimsoll line falls beneath the surface of the water, the vessel is in danger of tipping or sinking. Either result would be devastating, maybe deadly.

The Lord Jesus, our faithful High Priest, can sympathize with us in our weak moments, and He knows what our Plimsoll line is. He will not allow us to be tempted beyond our powers to resist. We can conquer temptation. We don't have to be overcome or consumed.

Temptations Are Escapable, Not Enclosing

The Lord has promised us a way of escape. Think of a pass through the mountains. You may feel surrounded or hemmed in, but God will provide an escape route. Perhaps the best advice is to avoid the mountains.

Joseph offers a classic example of how to escape. Day after day, he was approached by Potipher's wife, who had immorality on her mind. One day she caught Joseph all alone and pursued her evil intention. "Lie with me, Joseph," she said. "No one will ever know. Come on, Joseph. Let's have a little fun." But Joseph knew better and fled. Sometimes the most spiritual and manly thing you can do is run. In 1 Corinthians 10:14, Paul said, "Therefore, my beloved, flee from immorality." Joseph ran. He may have lost his cloak, but he maintained his character.

Good for Joseph! Way to go, Joey!

Temptations Are Passing, Not Permanent

Verse 13 ends by saying, "You will be able to endure it." The allure and attraction will pass. I think of the season of temptation in Jesus' life (Matthew 4). He was tempted by the devil on three noteworthy occasions, but verse 11 says, "The devil left him." Luke's gospel adds, "Until an opportune time" (4:13). It's important to remember that when it comes to temptation and other matters of spiritual warfare, the battles are never permanent, but neither are the peaceful times.

The words of 1 Corinthians 10 are examples and reminders for us. Never forget the lessons that Paul teaches: God is available (vv. 3–4) and God is faithful (v. 13). When temptation comes your way, remember that He still is!

But temptations.

Homestead, Florida

But Married Folks

1 Corinthians 7

I'm writing this chapter on the eve of my twenty-eighth wedding anniversary. I am a very blessed man. Admittedly, I married up, way over my head, and to use a football term, I've outkicked my coverage!

Not everyone shares my optimism. For many, marriage has become a three-ring circus. There's the engagement ring, the wedding ring, and then the suffering! As a pastor, I've met many people who desire to tie the knot, but honestly, they are not fit to be tied!

I wish this were a rare problem, but it seems more and more people are struggling in their marriages. You'd think this was true only of the unregenerate, but that's not the case. More than 50 percent of the marriages in our country end in divorce whether the couple is saved or lost, churched or unchurched.

I got a text message at six this morning followed by an hour-long phone call from a dear Christian lady whose marriage of twenty-plus years is in shambles and hanging on by a very thin thread. The husband and wife both profess the Lord. In fact, they have served in ministry. Friction, frustration, finances, and foolish decisions have now landed them in some mighty turbulent waters. I wish their case were isolated, but it's not. In fact, it's all too common.

Much of 1 Corinthians 7 deals with the relationship of a husband and wife. Paul wrote to the Corinthian church to offer counsel on how to have a happy, holy, healthy, and harmonious marriage. The text reads like an episode of Dr. Phil!

According to *Strong's Exhaustive Concordance of the Bible*, the word *but* is found twenty-five times in this chapter. Paul included it in his many admonitions to readers. This chapter is full of advice on marriage. What can we glean from Paul's words?

Come Together

Some in Corinth had begun to wonder if a life of celibacy was more spiritual than a married life. Paul explored this issue and wrote of the benefits of marital love.

Someone once asked me, "What are the reasons for marriage?" From a biblical standpoint, I see at least five:

(1.) Partnership (Genesis 2:18): God said it's not good for a man to be alone, and I agree!

(2.) Pleasure (Proverbs 5:18–19): The joys of sexual fulfillment are exclusively for a husband and a wife. The marriage bed should be held in honor.

(3.) Procreation (Genesis 1:28): God gave us the exhortation to be fruitful and to multiply. Children are indeed a gift from the Lord. Have a quiver full of them!

(4.) Purity (1 Corinthians 7:2): As a safeguard from temptation and sexual sin, Paul told the men to get a wife and the women to get a husband. Of course, being married doesn't mean that sexual temptation will no longer come your way.

(5.) Picture (Ephesians 5:22–23): Paul said that the husband and wife are an illustration of Christ (the groom) and His church (the bride). If for no other reason, that's why our marriages must be pure and rewarding.

I remind you to marry only a Christian. Further, pray that your future spouse (or those of your children or grandchildren) will be a growing believer whose spiritual life will be a challenge and an inspiration to you. It is also wise to marry a person of like faith and belief.

Be Together

Most of my pastoral counseling sessions over sexual issues involve extramarital affairs. In Corinth, some were avoiding the act of marriage with their spouses. In our sex-crazed society this doesn't seem to be as big an issue, but it is an issue for some.

Isn't it strange that teenagers and young adults seemingly can't keep their hands off of one another, but when they reach middle age they lose that drive?

In 1 Corinthians 7:1–5, 10–11, God tells us everything we need to know about intimacy in marriage. Note what He says.

- Reserve your affection for your spouse (vv. 1–2). Paul reminds us that God's plan is virginity before marriage and fidelity in marriage.
- Receive affection from your spouse (v. 3). We've now moved from the premarital stage to marriage. Husbands and wives must remember that they owe each other love and affection. One writer wisely said, "The bonds of matrimony will surely go into default if the interest is not kept up!"
- Release affection to your spouse (vv. 4–5). Here Paul offers a suggestion for practicing marital fidelity. When we marry we gain something but we also lose something. We gain a mate but we lose authority over our own bodies. So let's stop defrauding one another of sexual fulfillment!
- Retain your affection for your spouse (vv. 10–11). We are not to leave our spouse physically or withhold from them sexually, is the idea.

Stay Together

In my years of ministry, I've noticed two problems when it comes to marriage. People are too quick to jump in and to jump out! If you've ever wondered what the Bible says about marriage, divorce, or remarriage, a basic summary is found in 1 Corinthians 7.

What a sad state we are in when every other marriage ends in divorce. No one profits from divorce but attorneys. The family doesn't benefit. The children don't benefit. The local church doesn't benefit. The community doesn't benefit. Only lawyers do!

So, whether you are married now or hope to be one day, jump into this chapter before you jump into marriage or into bed. A television talk show recently had as a guest an actor well known for playing romantic roles. The host asked him a probing question, "What makes a great lover?" The studio audience and all those watching on television expected some off-color, macho remark. To the surprise of everyone, the actor said, "A great lover is someone who can satisfy his spouse her whole life long, and can be satisfied by her all his life. A great lover is not someone who goes from woman to woman to woman. Any flea-infested dog can do that." That's a biblical and worthwhile response.

But married folks.

Lancaster, Virginia

But Be Filled with the Holy Spirit

Ephesians 5:15–21

Of all the chapters in this book, this one may be the most crucial and the most needed. I believe that the answer for America, the hope for our hearts, and the medicine for our marriages are found in the Spirit-filled life—that is, having a relationship with Jesus and relying on the resources of the Holy Spirit. The answer is Jesus.

Years ago, I told the story of a pastor speaking to a group of junior boys. He was trying to relate to them and to be relevant. Finally, he asked them a question, "Boys, what is gray, furry, has a long tail, eats nuts, and climbs trees?" Hands popped up all around the room. "Johnny, what is it?" the pastor said. "Well," Johnny replied, "I know the answer has to be Jesus, but it sounds like a squirrel to me."

The truth is, the answer to all of life's dilemmas has to be Jesus.

The epistle to the Ephesians is a favorite among pastors and laypersons alike. It begins in a theological vein but ends up being quite practical.

Paul uses an illustration from everyday life that surely gets readers' attention. The illustration deals with being drunk on wine. The way a person gets drunk is by drinking, and the way a person stays drunk is by continuing to drink. This is an illustration, not an endorsement.

I'm not a drinker. I used to be before I met Jesus. When I finally drank from the Lord's well, none of the drinks of the world would satisfy. There was a day when alcohol was not tolerated in our churches or among our members. I'm what we once called a teetotaler. I wish everyone else were too!

It's funny (sad really) that the only two Bible verses some Baptists know are "Judge not lest you be judged" (Matthew 7:1) and "Drink no longer water only, but use a little wine for the stomach's sake and thine often infirmities" (1 Timothy 5:23). I'm afraid the problem is not our stomach. It's our heart!

Take a moment and meditate on our text (Ephesians 5:15–21), and we'll examine two entirely different sources and outcomes.

Do Not Get Drunk with Wine

I've been around long enough to hear all the arguments for and against the consumption of alcoholic beverages. Here is what I believe: drinking will deceive your friends, destroy your family, and diminish your faith. When people begin to compromise in this area or any other, they will rationalize all of their poor choices.

Note what Paul writes here:

Be careful how you walk.
Walk not as unwise men but as wise.
Make the most of your time.
Don't waste opportunities.
Do not be foolish.
Live to do God's will.

How in the world can any of us seek to observe these admonitions and at the same time justify our alcohol use? Wake up, people! We know better than that. We must always rely on the principles in God's Word and not on men's opinions or on popularity polls.

I don't pretend to be a Greek scholar or an expert linguist, but there are two terms in verse 18 that need further explanation. W. E. Vine is a recognized name among students of Greek. In his helpful work *Vine's Expository Dictionary of New Testament Words* (Iowa Falls,

Iowa: Riverside Book and Bible House), he says that *get drunk* (in the Greek, *methusko*) signifies to be drunk, to make drunk, or to grow in drunkenness. This word is an inceptive verb, marking the process of the state expressed. Literally, Paul is saying, do not begin the process of becoming intoxicated. That process begins with your first beer, your first shot, your first glass of wine, or your first martini. That's why I'm a teetotaler.

The second term, *dissipation* or *excess*, is *asotia* in the Greek. This word is also translated as "riot." *Asotia* is from *a* (a negative) and *sozo*, "to save" (from which comes the idea of soteriology, or the doctrine of salvation. The alpha *a* in the Greek text is like the *un* in the English text. It reverses or negates a situation. You could translate this word as "unsaved" or "unsalvation." I affirm this approach.

Now go back and put the expanded ideas of verse 18 together. The verse would then read, "And do not begin the process of becoming intoxicated, for that is unsalvation, the kind of thing unsaved people do. Instead, be filled with and controlled by the Holy Spirit of God." As Abraham Lincoln said, "Alcohol has many defenders, but truly it has no defense." Enough said. I'll get off of my soapbox for now!

Be Filled with the Holy Spirit

Instead of being filled with and under the control of alcohol, we are to be filled with the Holy Spirit and under the Spirit's control. Every aspect of a believer's life should be dominated by the Holy Spirit. The word *filled* is in the imperative mood. That means we as Christians are commanded to keep being filled and to stay filled. The reason we need to keep being filled is because we keep leaking!

Paul uses the balance of Ephesians to show that the Christian living a life dominated by the Holy Spirit can be beneficial and successful.

The Holy Spirit will aid your worship life (5:19–21).

The Holy Spirit will aid your wedded life (5:22–6:4).

The Holy Spirit will aid your work life (6:5–9). A key for successful employers and employees is a Spirit-controlled life.

The Holy Spirit will aid your war life (6:10–18). Spiritual battles cannot be won by fleshly means.

The Holy Spirit will aid your witness life (6:18–20). Acts 4:31 says, "And when they had prayed, the place where they had gathered together was shaken, and they were all filled with the Holy Spirit, and they began to speak the word of God with boldness."

If you and I want continued success and satisfaction in life, we must stay full of and controlled by the Holy Spirit.

But be filled with the Holy Spirit.

Assisi, Italy

But God

Ephesians 2:4

According to one online search engine, the phrase *but God* is found in the Scripture sixty-one times. Expanded uses of these words or this idea would certainly produce many additional instances. These are two words of monumental importance.

For the past thirty days, we have noticed the word *but* connected with a person, a group of people, or a circumstance—but Noah, but Daniel, but Jonah, but married folks, but Judas, just to mention a few. All are good and challenging, but today's hinge is the best of all: "but God."

I will note five of the uses of this phrase in the Bible.

"*But God* demonstrates His own love toward us, in that while we were yet sinners, Christ died for us" (Romans 5:8).

God did more for us than just declare or discuss His love. He demonstrated it. He showed us how much He loved us by giving His only Son to die in our place. God didn't do this because we deserved it. We were still sinners living in our sin. Perhaps the most beloved verse in the Bible says, "For God so loved the world that He gave His only begotten Son, that whosoever believes in Him will not perish but have everlasting life" (John 3:16). God's love landed Christ on the cross, but it can land us in heaven.

"*But God*, being rich in mercy, because of His great love with which He loved us, even when we were dead in our transgressions, made us alive together with Christ" (Ephesians 2:4–5).

The opening chapters of Ephesians are filled with theological truth and significance. The second chapter begins by saying we are spiritually dead (v. 1) but that God made us alive (vv. 4–5). This afternoon my pastoral duties brought me to a hospital to visit a dear lady from my church. While I was there, it became obvious that things were not well in the room next door. I could see the crowd, hear the cries, and watch the expressions. A man named Billy had just died. The family asked me to pray, but Billy was gone.

When people die, they have no awareness, no ability, and no appetite. It doesn't matter if they've been dead for seventeen seconds, seventeen minutes, seventeen days, or seventeen years; when they're dead, they're dead.

There will be various levels of decay but not of death.

The only hope for a dead person is Jesus. Whether someone is physically dead (as Lazarus was) or spiritually dead, that person needs a *but God* moment. Ephesians 2 describes a bad situation (vv. 1–3) and a glorious salvation (vv. 8–10).

"When they had carried out all that was written concerning Him, they took Him down from the cross and laid Him in a tomb. *But God* raised Him from the dead" (Acts 13:29–30).

In the same way God has given us spiritual life, He physically raised Christ. In this passage, the apostle Paul shares the gospel story. He speaks of Christ's life, death, and resurrection. Man put Him in the tomb, *but God* raised Him from the dead. What good is a dead God? Thanks be to God for His resurrection!

"I planted, Apollos watered, *but God* was causing the growth. So then neither the one who plants nor the one who waters is anything, *but God* who causes the growth" (1 Corinthians 3:6–7).

Here Paul reminded the Corinthian church of his ministry and of what God does. Paul used an agricultural metaphor in discussing foundations, planting, and harvesting.

The point is that there is much all of us can and should do in ministry and service for our Lord and His church, but we must constantly be reminded that it is God who causes the growth.

"As for you, you meant evil against me, *but God* meant it for good in order to bring about this present result, to preserve many people alive" (Genesis 50:20).

I hope you know this verse and it's setting well. It has been called the Romans 8:28 of the Old Testament. Here is why.

Joseph's brothers, out of envy and resentment, sought to do him harm. They sold him to a caravan of Ishmaelites for twenty shekels of silver. The Ishmaelites brought Joseph to Egypt—right where God wanted him. His brothers meant to do him evil, *but God* had other plans, and He always wins out!

You may not understand what is happening to you or to your family, your ministry, or your church. It may appear that the world, the flesh, and the devil are going to win out. Wait! Perhaps there is a *but God* moment in your future.

Lest you think all of that is just theological rhetoric or preacher talk, I need those *but God* scenarios too. Some things have happened in my family today that require God's intervention. The situation looks pretty grim. I'm praying. I'm hoping. I'm trusting. But God!

I'm reminded of the words of the psalmist, "My heart and flesh may fail, *but God* is the strength of my heart and my portion forever" (Psalm 73:26).

But God.

Conclusion

In each of this book's thirty-one chapters, my focus has been on the little word *but*. Over and again in Scripture, that word represents a turning point. Something has happened, but ... a person has acted, but ...

I have referred to this word as a small hinge on which a big door swings. I want to end by shifting our focus from the hinge to the door. *The Door.*

Jesus Is the Door (John 10:7, 9)

Unless you're a cowboy or a rancher, you may not understand the analogy. Shepherds in biblical times would pick up on this metaphor quickly. They would build a fold for their sheep as a way to gather and protect them. Wild dogs were common. David spoke of a lion and a bear.

Once the shepherd had accounted for all of his sheep, he would stand at or lie over the one opening. He wasn't just at the door; he was the door. This is the picture Christ gives us in John 10.

Have you been through the door? Have you entered God's fold by placing your faith in Jesus? If not, I pray you do that even now!

Jesus Stands at the Door (Revelation 3:20)

The church at Laodicea was one Christ spoke of in Revelation. Members of this church were going through the motions of religious duty and filling the calendar with "spiritual" activity. They were doing this without the Lord. According to verse 20, Jesus had been pushed out of His own church. Can you imagine? Now He was standing at the door, knocking. He wanted back in.

The church continued with its busy schedule of events, but Jesus was not there. I think I've attended that kind of church before. Have you?

Have you gotten away from Christ, His church, or His amazing plan? Have you pushed or crowded Jesus out of your life? Is your quiet time stale? Does your prayer life lack power? If so, I invite you to return in a fresh way to the Lord. He is knocking and He wants so much to be admitted back into your life. Will you open the door?

Jesus Provided an Open Door (Revelation 3:8)

Many historians and theologians believe that each of the seven churches of Asia Minor was not only a local assembly, but represented a unique facet of the church's development. If so, the church at Philadelphia represented the church's missionary spirit. It was to this assembly that Jesus said, "I've set before you an open door."

In other words, the time is now to encourage missions, mission development, mission trips, mission offerings, and the sending of missionaries. Why is that important? Why do we do that? Because God has set before us an open door! Opportunities abound all around us to take the gospel to the ends of the earth. Missiologists tell us that as many as two billion people still have no consistent gospel witness. We must go to all the world for Jesus' sake!

So as you begin to observe these hinges, don't overlook the doors attached to them. I trust you will see that *Big Doors Swing on Small Hinges.*

Your Next Step

Now that you've read the book, *Big Doors Swing on Small Hinges*, I invite you to follow me on twitter, facebook, and go to my homepage www.rogermardis.com. Here you can follow my blog, keep up with my schedule/speaking events, book signings, and learn more about me and my amazing family. I hope you'll visit us soon.

You can also learn more about Agape Baptist – Scottsboro by visiting www.agapebaptist.com.

Finally, be looking for my next book due out in 2016, 31 *Amazing Ships of the Bible*.

CPSIA information can be obtained at www.ICGtesting.com
Printed in the USA
LVOW11s2025110614

389615LV00001B/1/P